C000065177

Edinburgh Airport

A HISTORY

Edinburgh Airport
A HISTORY

KEITH McCLOSKEY

TEMPUS

Dedication

For my son,
Michael Liam McCloskey,
who shared my love of aviation.
20.8.1979 – 9.12.2004

Frontispiece:
Above: Channel Airways Scottish Flyer Viscount,
August 1969. (G.W. Sheridan)
Below: Flybe Bombardier Dash 8Q-402 powers
up for take off. Based at Exeter, Flybe is now one
of Europe's largest independent low-fare airlines.
(Glenn Surtees)

First published 2006

Tempus Publishing Limited
The Mill, Brimscombe Port,
Stroud, Gloucestershire, GL5 2QG
www.tempus-publishing.com

© Keith McCloskey, 2006

The right of Keith McCloskey to be identified as the Author
of this work has been asserted in accordance with the
Copyrights, Designs and Patents Act 1988.

All rights reserved. No part of this book may be reprinted
or reproduced or utilised in any form or by any electronic,
mechanical or other means, now known or hereafter invented,
including photocopying and recording, or in any information
storage or retrieval system, without the permission in writing
from the Publishers.

British Library Cataloguing in Publication Data.
A catalogue record for this book is available from the British Library.

ISBN 0 7524 3805 0
Typesetting and origination by Tempus Publishing Limited
Printed in Great Britain

Contents

It is hoped to attract more long-haul services like this Continental Airines Boeing 757-224/ET N14115, landing from New York Newark. (Joe Curry)

Air Zaire DC 10-30 9Q-CLI, named Mont Ngaliema (after the area accommodating the Marble Palace of President Mobutu), 6 May 1980. A most unusual visitor to the British Isles, let alone Edinburgh. Air Zaire went bankrupt in 1994. (Robert Pittuck)

Foreword

The story of the efforts to provide Scotland's capital city with a first-class airport is not an inspiring one. The late 1920s and 1930s saw a period of hesitancy, argument and prevarication. It is wrongly assumed by many people that Turnhouse was always the airport for Edinburgh, but this is not the case. The RAF Aerodrome became the civil airport for Edinburgh in 1947 almost by default after a long period of uncertainty up to the start of the Second World War.

After a distinguished record in both wars, the opening of RAF Turnhouse in 1947 for civil flights saw more seeming disinterest from central authorities, leading to a stoppage of the connection with London in the winter of 1947–48. Despite the provision of a new terminal in 1956, the continual growth in passengers and services led to the facilities at the airport becoming totally inadequate by the 1960s and this, in addition to the problems caused by a badly aligned main runway, resulted in large numbers of cancellations and diversions. From around 1962–63 until the BAA takeover in 1971, the argument went back and forth between all the various parties involved as to who was going to pay to improve the airport. Press cuttings from this period have headlines like 'Cinderella Airport', 'Possibly the Worst Airport in Europe', 'No Surveillance Radar'. Page after page of it.

Nobody would call it a 'Cinderella Airport' now, but the provision of first-class facilities was a long time coming and it took the BAA to have the will to carry it out.

With this history I have attempted to cater for the general reader as well as the enthusiast. Many people are put off by exhaustive lists of registrations and serial numbers and exact aircraft models. I have included these where I felt they were relevant. Equally no book on the history of the airport could be written without including RAF Turnhouse and the military side. This really deserves a book on its own and I have given a pen portrait of military matters with the emphasis on 603 (City of Edinburgh) Squadron. The sources section has details of the main work on 603 Squadron.

Considering that it is now thirty-six years since I first set foot on the Spectators' Terrace at the old original terminal building, it surprised me that no-one had written a full history of the airport.

As for many of us in this line, I have very fond memories of the airport. I spent many happy years there watching the aircraft. Equally, whenever I was travelling and the Viscount, Vanguard, Trident, BAC 1–11, Boeing 737 or 757 touched down at Edinburgh, I felt as if I had arrived safely home. It seemed a fitting tribute to write a book about the gateway to the city. Long may it prosper!

NB: The airport was and is still called Turnhouse by many people. After the BAA takeover it was promoted as Edinburgh Airport. This has been the practice with many UK airports as the names were usually taken from nearby villages or towns (Manchester International Airport was formerly called Ringway, while Durham Tees Valley Airport was once known as Middleton St George, for example). For the sake of good order I have used both Turnhouse and Edinburgh up to the BAA takeover and only Edinburgh (Airport) after that.

A KMV TU-204 arrives, bringing football supporters from the Ukraine. (Glenn Surtees)

Acknowledgements

I would like to particularly acknowledge the following people, without whom this book could not have been completed:

Squadron Leader Bruce Blanche QVRM AE BSc MSc DIC FGS RAuxAF (Ret.), RAuxAF Historian/Archivist: Squadron Leader Bruce Blanche has served with 603 Squadron and is the official historian for the squadron. In addition to providing information on 603, Bruce has also provided invaluable help with the history of the airport, checking my first manuscript as well as providing photographs. For anyone wishing to carry out research on the RAuxAF and 603 Squadron, I would recommend Bruce as your first port of call.

Len Houston: Len was with the Ferranti Flying Unit from 1956 to 1973 and was their chief test pilot (from 1964 to 1973). He very kindly prepared the section on the Ferranti Flying Unit along with the FFU appendix details and photographs for which I am deeply indebted.

Jim O'Sullivan: I am a technophobe and, besides taking some of the photographs, Jim has looked after the technical aspects and preparation of the photographs for the book.

Colin Lourie: As stated in the 'Sources' section, Colin runs an excellent 1960s Turnhouse website and kindly opened up his large collection of photographs from that era to the 1980s/1990s (a collection which, for that period, is probably unequalled) to use in the book, for which I am indebted.

I would also like to thank the following for their help in the preparation of the book:

British Airways Museum (Paul Jarvis (Manager), Keith Hayward, Jim Davis, Howell Green, Doug Cotterell, Gill Sparrow); John Rowley; Mark Lander; Scott Mcintosh; Sandy Benzies; Ian Stott; Peter Ward; Colonel Jon Peder Ryste (Defence attaché, Royal Norwegian Embassy, London); Colonel Bruno Maurice (Air attaché, Embassy of France, London); Allen McLaughlin; W. Dunbar; Anne Morrison (Edinburgh Room, George IV Library, Edinburgh), who always had books and documents at the ready on my visits to the library; Helen Osmani (Image Licensing & Product Dev. Manager, Nat. Museums of Scotland); Flight Lieutenant Harrison (603 Squadron); Gary Brindle; Glenn Surtees; Harry Shinkfield and Mike Varley for information on 77 Squadron; Gemma Whitman for help on Concorde details; Rachel Cameron (BAA Edinburgh); Gordon Pearson; Robert Pittuck; Anne Follin (Manager Planning & Development, BAA Edinburgh); Raymond Wang; Iain Hutchison for a lot of help on both early and later Scottish aviation as well as advice on the manuscript; Guy Warner for reading and checking the final manuscript plus helping with information on services and aircraft and general guidance; Peter Crouch (European Aeronautical Group UK Ltd); Haynes Sutton Publishing; Alistair Robertson for advice on Scottish Air Cargo; Susan Courtney and Debbie McLean (Civil Aviation Authority); *Flight International* (article on Grangemouth Airport, 6 July 1939); Bob Graham (Edinburgh Flying Club); Fleet Air Arm Museum (for information on FAA squadrons at Turnhouse); Norrie Simpson; Richard Wainwright (BAA) for providing information and removing a major headache for me at the last minute with statistics; Alexander Crawford for guidance on 263 Squadron; Martin Krupka; Alexander J. Cunningham; Iain Duncan–Smith MP for details of his early life at Turnhouse and also details of his father; Dougal McIntyre for sharing his unrivalled knowledge and kind donation of the Grangemouth photograph plus advice and direction; Alistair Dickson; Neil Geddes; Jim Fulton for a lot of help on details; Gordon S. Sandford (NATS) for help on 1980s services and providing photographs; Stuart Leslie; David Ross for pictures of 603 Squadron at Turnhouse and welcome advice; Forbes Ingils (RAF Montrose Aviation Heritage Museum); Lizzie Platt & Grub Street publishers for their kind permission for 603 Squadron material and photographs to be used from *The Greatest Squadron of Them All*; Peter Hewitt, Flight Crew Manager, British Midland, for information on British Midland (plus a comfortable flight to Edinburgh in an A321); Stephen Muir for operational information (BAA Ops Edinburgh); Kevin Lang (BAA Edinburgh); Squadron Leader Douglas Tidy; Keith Meakin (Gen. Manager NATS); Peter Gibson for the final word on the FFU; Sandra Dick and Kerry Black (*Scotsman/Edinburgh Evening News*); 'RIP Concorde' (from Airliner World Commercial Forum); John Binge (FAST Farnborough); J. Bricknall; Mike Jenvy; former Trident pilot Peter Whittle for his description of Trident landings and take-offs on the old 13/31 (now 12/30) main runway at Edinburgh; The Rt Hon. The Earl of Rosebery for providing background information relating to his grandfather's dispute with the Ministry of Munitions over the ownership of Turnhouse; Charlie Durnford (ex-RAF and Scottish Fisheries) for providing the information and photographs for the section on Scottish Fisheries; Martina Caspers (Bundesarchiv, Koblenz); Wilhelm Ratuszynski; J.B. Cynk; Colonel Marek Lisiak (Defence Section, Polish Embassy, London); John Hayles for information on Aquila Airways; Squadron Leader Vince Butler and Flight Lt Davis, RAF Leuchars (for information on 12 AEF and ELUAS); Niall Corduroy; Phil Vigor (BAA); Alison Smith-Reilly (BAA); Ben Brown; Bill Sheridan; Linda Rudd; Mrs K.E.M. O'Sullivan for help with the preparation of the manuscript and, last but not least, my daughter Camilla for the use of her computer, phone and endless tea.

Extracts from Norman & Dawbarn 'Report on a land airport for the city of Edinburgh' reproduced by kind permission of Capita Norman & Dawbarn.

References and extracts from 1967 study by Fettes pupils reproduced by kind permission of the Headmaster of Fettes College.

1

The Beginning

Edinburgh's civil airport, in contrast to other UK and European airports, got off to a rather slow start. The eventual location, Turnhouse, actually started life as a Flight Station of the Aeroplane Barrage Line in 1915. In 1916 the airfield was used as a training centre with Maurice Farman Shorthorns and Longhorns. Both aircraft were fitted with 'pusher engines' and were very early designs, although the Shorthorn (officially known as the Maurice Farman S.11) was fitted with dual controls and adequately fulfilled its various roles as a reconnaissance, bomber and trainer aircraft. The first aircraft received at the aerodrome arrived on 22 May 1916 when 26 Reserve Squadron RFC (Royal Flying Corps – the forerunner of the Royal Air Force) was formed as a training squadron. The aircraft were sheltered in canvas hangars but the first permanent hangar was built later that year. Turnhouse was home to 26 Squadron until 22 September when they moved to Harlaxton. B Flight of 36 (Home Defence) Squadron arrived from Cramlington in May 1916 and stayed until 12 October 1916 when they moved to Hylton.

Although there were many air raids by German Zeppelins between January 1915 and August 1918 on Yorkshire, the Midlands and the North East, there was actually only one raid on Edinburgh. This was on the night of 2/3 April 1916, when a total of forty-seven bombs were dropped on the city and thirteen people were killed. Air protection of the city was introduced after this raid but there were no further attacks. No.77 Squadron of the RFC was formed in Edinburgh on 1 October 1916 as a home defence unit and was commanded by Major W. Milne MC. The thistle in the squadron crest commemorates the formation of 77 Squadron in Scotland. In addition to the defence of the city, the squadron was also given responsibility for defending the Firth of Forth against nocturnal Zeppelin raids, asked to co-operate with the Forth garrison batteries and the Scottish Command in case of enemy landings, and expected to train night-flying pilots for overseas operations. Three flights of the Squadron were based in the area flying from airfields at New Haggerston, Whitburn and Penston and were equipped with BE2C, BE2E, BE12 and BE12B single engine fighter aircraft, none of which were really suitable for the tasks they had been given.

The BE aircraft have been rather unjustly criticised, as they were designed with stability in mind, and were not successful in the fighter roles to which they were assigned. Many considered the aircraft obsolete, and believed that too much was expected of them.

Wight seaplane type 840 at Granton harbour, 1915, after delivery from Dalmuir. (Stuart Leslie/Fleet Air Arm Museum)

On 13 April 1917, 77 Squadron moved to Turnhouse. They suffered their first casualty almost immediately after they arrived. Lieutenant David Steven-Gibson of the Black Watch, who also flew in the RFC, was killed in a flying accident on 17 April 1917 when the BE12A fighter he was ferrying from London to Turnhouse crashed at Knaresborough in the West Riding of Yorkshire. He had landed the BE12A in thick fog on a cricket field. After the fog cleared, he attempted to take off, but the wheels of the aircraft hit a stone or rut which jerked it up into the air. The aircraft hit trees, and was catapulted into the river Nidd. The body of Lieutenant Steven-Gibson was found three weeks later but, oddly, no trace of the aircraft was ever found. Flying during the First World War was a considerable hazard, and there is a strong likelihood of other crashes, but without loss of life, during the period No.77 Squadron was based at Turnhouse. Records for this period are few and far between, and official reports of crashes are not forthcoming.

The commander of No.77 Squadron at this time was Major van der Spey, who was replaced in September 1917 by Major Summervail who had been wounded in the Turkish campaign in the Dardenelles.

Two Canadian Squadrons formed at Turnhouse in early 1917. January 1917 saw the formation of 84 Reserve Squadron (Can), before the squadron moved on to northern Toronto in February. A little later, on 15 March, 89 Reserve Squadron (Can) was formed, but was transferred to Beverley on 18 April.

A detachment of 26 Training Squadron (B Flight) was briefly at Turnhouse from 20 July to 31 July 1917 before moving to Wittering/Stamford, while No.73 (Training) Squadron moved to Turnhouse from Thetford with Sopwith Camels on 17 September

Turnhouse, 1916: mixed hangar types with Sopwith Camels. (Stuart Leslie/Fleet Air Arm Museum)

77 Squadron, early 1918: a mixture of Avro 504s and BE12Bs. (Photograph supplied by FAST Photo Archive)

77 Squadron, early 1918: a mixture of Avro 504s and BE12Bs. (Photograph supplied by FAST Photo Archive)

77 Squadron Group photograph, early 1918: many of the squadron's officers came from Scottish regiments. (Photograph supplied by FAST Photo Archive)

1917 before moving to Beaulieu on 20 February 1918. Approximately 6,000 Sopwith Camels were produced, and they were credited with shooting down 1,294 enemy aircraft. Although the Camel was considered to be an agile fighter aircraft in the right hands, it was notoriously difficult to fly. Depending on the degree of skill of the pilot, the Camel was said to offer a choice between a wooden cross, the Red Cross or the Victoria Cross.

In January 1918, 77 Squadron was re-equipped with the Avro 504K which was modified for night-flying. Like the BE2 and BE12, the Avro 504K was ill-suited to the role of a front-line fighter and was more often used as a trainer. In April 1918, the squadron moved to Penston and, following the Armistice, it was gradually run down until it was disbanded on 13 June 1919.

After the departure of 73 and 77 Squadrons, the aerodrome became a Fleet Aeroplane Base, coming directly under the command of the Commander-in-Chief of the Grand Fleet. Turnhouse ceased being a fleet aircraft base in 1919 and was later used as a fleet aircraft repair depot and practice station. For a while, the aerodrome was home to 104 Squadron. The squadron had previously been stationed at Maisoncelle, France, and, after a brief time at Turnhouse, left for Crail on 3 March 1919.

By the end of the First World War, Turnhouse Aerodrome covered 149 acres with a landing strip measuring 1550 x 450 yards. There was one Home Defence pattern hangar unit of 130ft x 120ft, two 1915 pattern hangars measuring 200ft x 70ft, one 1915 pattern hangar of 150ft x 70ft, and one 1916 pattern hangar of 170ft x 80ft. The land on which

77 Squadron Avro 504, early 1918. (Photograph supplied by FAST Photo Archive)

77 Squadron BE12B, early 1918. (Photograph supplied by FAST Photo Archive)

Turnhouse was built adjoined the Dalmeny Estate (which had been in the family of the Earl of Rosebery since 1665) and Turnhouse Farm and Craigiehall, which had been bought by the then earl of Rosebery (a former Prime Minister) for his son in 1915. The son unfortunately died in 1917. The land was commandeered by the Ministry of Munitions at the outbreak of the First World War for use as an aerodrome. Towards the end of November 1919 controversy arose when the ministry offered Turnhouse Farm and Turnhouse Aerodrome and 178¼ acres of land 'for disposal as a whole, or the buildings and the land on which they stand'. There was an angry response to this from the Earl who carried out a war of words through the pages of *The Scotsman*.

His first letter to *The Scotsman* pointed out that the land was his and that the ministry had no right to offer it for sale. The Permanent Under-Secretary, Sir Howard Frank, replied on 1 December 1919, stating that the government was within its rights to purchase the land and: 'To secure to the taxpayer as large a return as possible for expenditure necessitated by the war, and to avoid the waste involved in the destruction of expensive buildings which may be of permanent utility for industrial or other purposes'. A series of letters from both sides followed, with the tone becoming increasingly acrimonious. On 12 December, Rosebery wrote a letter to the newspaper stating:

> ...to me I confess it is a matter of indifference, if I am to be robbed, whether it is by a pickpocket or a burglar. You have, as you well know, no equitable claim or title to Turnhouse. And to sell my best farm to recoup your department's wasteful expenditure is an unscrupulous depredation unworthy of any minister. I have been a minister myself, and should have blushed to countenance such malpractices. You seem to glory in them...

Sopwith Camel B6304 30 Wing ARS Turnhouse. (Stuart Leslie/Fleet Air Arm Museum)

Two Sopwith Camel 2F1s, N7149 Swillington and N7146 Lt. McLeod Test Flight ARS Turnhouse.
(Stuart Leslie/Fleet Air Arm Museum)

In a further letter to *The Scotsman* on 16 December Rosebery continued his criticism
of Frank, stating:

> You claim without a blush to protect the taxpayer. It is from you, however, that he needs
> protection, you who have spent £68,000 on these squalid huts. No wonder you wish to
> hide this extravagance. What I complain of is that you wish to hide it at my expense.

On the 17 December Sir Howard withdrew from the exchange, stating:

> I have no intention of replying to the personal attacks you have made on me... This
> correspondence is closed so far as I am concerned.

The incident was closed, eventually, the final say on the matter coming from Rosebery, in
his letter to *The Times*, 18 December. The disagreement was presumably resolved to the
satisfaction of both parties. Rosebery had 100 copies of the complete correspondence
of the affair printed under the title *Turnhouse: An Object Lesson.*

DH9A E8515 with hydrovanes and wingtip floats, delivered to Turnhouse on 24 October 1918. It was disposed of in January 1919. (Stuart Leslie/Fleet Air Arm Museum)

2
Interwar

Turnhouse had always been considered a military aerodrome, and various sites around Edinburgh were used for civilian flying (including, from time to time, Turnhouse itself). There were several squadrons based at Turnhouse over the years, but 603 Squadron is particularly worthy of mention, being Edinburgh's own. On 12 October 1925, the Air Ministry issued the following order (Air Order 1611):

> It is notified for information and necessary action by all concerned that an auxiliary Air Force, No.603 City of Edinburgh (Bombing) Squadron is to commence to form at Turnhouse on 14 October 1925, in accordance with Establishment No.AAF/501.
>
> The Squadron is ultimately to be provided with aircraft to the establishment of a regular single-engine bombing squadron, but it has been decided that on formation the Squadron will have a reduced establishment of aeroplanes to consist of: Four Avros, Six DH9As and two Dual DH9As.

The approved number of personnel for the squadron was set at twenty-three officers and 158 airmen. The squadron was formed under the command of Squadron Leader J.A. 'Jimmy' McKelvie AFC who was a veteran of the Royal Flying Corps and had flown Bristol Fighters with 22 Squadron during the First World War, attaining the rank of Major. The air correspondent of *The Scotsman*, Mr A. Scott Kennedy wrote in the newspaper on 25 October 1925:

> Major 'Jimmy' McKelvie... is to command the new Edinburgh bomber squadron – No.603, Auxiliary Air Force. An excellent choice, I have known him for a long time in and out of the service. The aircraft at Turnhouse, he tells me, are two Avro504Ks and one DH9A. I fancy it won't be long before his 'stable' is bigger. I am glad he has invited to help me with recruiting.

The 603 City of Edinburgh (Bombing) Squadron was formed as part of the Royal Air Force Auxiliary at Turnhouse on 14 October 1925 and it soon won the enthusiastic support of the people of Edinburgh. There were always far more applications than vacancies for both flying and ground posts. The squadron established its town HQ at

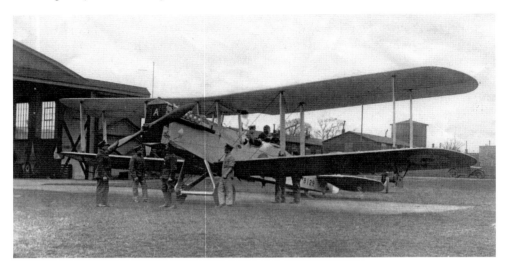

DH9A at Turnhouse, *c.*1928. (Squadron Leader Bruce Blanche Collection)

25 Learmonth Terrace near the centre of Edinburgh. Purchased for £4,500 from the wine merchant and whisky distiller Arthur Sanderson, the building has always been occupied by one or another of the city's RAF Auxiliary units (apart from during the war when it was occupied by the Air Training Corps). For training purposes, one Avro 504K was replaced by the Lynx engine type 504N in December 1926. By the end of 1927 all the old 'Mono Avros' had been replaced by the Lynx.

In 1928 a wireless station for air – ground communication was built. On 15 June of that year, an Imperial Airways Armstrong Whitworth Argosy (G–EBLF), named *City of Glasgow*, flown by Captain G.P. Olley, landed at Turnhouse at the end of its race against the LNER train *Flying Scotsman*, both having set off from London. The Argosy (carrying eighteen passengers) won, landing at Turnhouse 15 minutes ahead of the train, having stopped twice on the way for refuelling.

On the 7 July 1928 tragedy was to strike 603 Squadron, when pilot officer J.T.L. Shiells was killed in a flying accident going solo in the vicinity of Corstorphine. He had been a keen fencer, and a group of fellow officers had already organised an annual Shiells Fencing Trophy Cup for fencing competition. His parents also donated a sum of money in order that a Shiells Trophy for competition in areas other than fencing could be established in his honour. This was 603 Squadron's first fatality. The second came on 3 August 1930, when another accident claimed the life of Flt Lt A.R.H. Miller. Unfortunately there were to be many more deaths before the end of the war.

The squadron re-equipped with Westland Wapitis in March 1930 and was to re-equip with Hawker Harts in February 1934. Hawker Hinds arrived exactly four years later. These were replaced by Gloster Gladiator MkIs in March 1939, followed by Spitfire MkIs in September 1939. Aircraft were upgraded much faster than they are today!

A local landowner, Mr Paton, generously allowed his land on the Belstane Estate to be used as a bombing range by the squadron. The sudden death of Mr Paton in 1932 left the squadron without a practice range, so the new CO (Squadron Leader Hylton Murray-Philipson) generously allowed the use of his estate at Stobo near Peebles.

There had been talk of providing a civil airport for the City of Edinburgh up until 1932. On 25 May 1932, the Edinburgh Lord Provost's Committee discussed the issue and instructed the town clerk to find out what other cities had done about providing municipal airports. Nothing came from this and the matter dragged on. Up to this point various possible sites had been suggested, including Davidson's Mains, Silverknowes and Gilmerton.

On 22 March 1934, London, Scottish & Provincial Airways Ltd announced that they were planning a twice-daily service between London and Edinburgh with aircraft 'which were capable of travelling at 150 miles an hour' presumably referring to their two Airspeed Couriers (G–ACSY & G–ACSZ). They were going to employ 'the best pilots obtainable' and were to charge £5 for a single journey with a reduction for a return ticket. The London airport was to have been Croydon with stops at Nottingham and Manchester. It was intended that Turnhouse was to be used as the Edinburgh airport despite the fact that it was purely a military aerodrome at this stage. Unfortunately, the project never got off the ground, figuratively and literally. London, Scottish & Provincial had examined the possibility of also operating a London–Nottingham–Manchester–Renfrew service but decided against this and the London–Edinburgh route.

A service from Dyce to Turnhouse using DH84 Dragon G–ACAN (flown by Captain Eric Starling) was started by Aberdeen Airways on 4 June 1935. However, there were no passengers carried on the first round trip and the service was halted on 3 August 1935,

A Hawker Hart of 603 Squadron in unfortunate circumstances, 1930s. (Squadron Leader Bruce Blanche Collection)

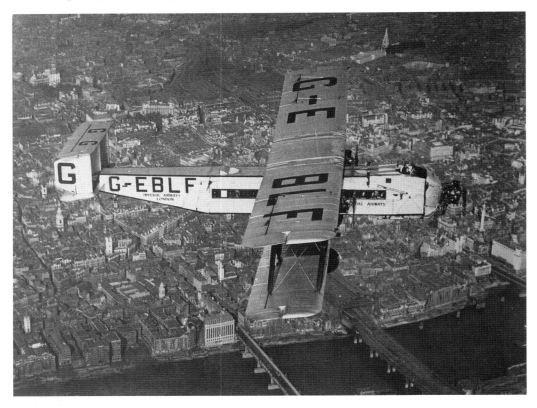

Imperial Airways Armstrong Whitworth Argosy. Although not an aerodynamic-looking shape, G–EBLF was the aircraft which beat the *Flying Scotsman* (by 15 minutes) in the race to Edinburgh from London in 1928. (A.J. Jackson Collection & Brooklands Museum)

with occasional 'on demand' services until summer 1936. There had been plans to link up with a London–Turnhouse service by North Eastern Airways, but this proved fruitless. In April 1935 North Eastern Airways began a twice-weekly service from Heston to Leeds and Newcastle, one of which went on to Edinburgh using Airspeed Envoys. The flight was 2¾ hours and the cost was £5 18s 6d and £9 9s return. This was another short-lived service.

This saga seemed to represent all attempts at providing a civil airport and air services for Edinburgh throughout the 1920s and 19
30s up until after the Second World War. The residents of Edinburgh seemed to show a keen interest in flying in the 1930s. An 'Air Circus' or 'Flying Day' was held at Maybury by SMT Aircraft, with three DH Dragons, six Fox Moths, four Avro Cadets and one Tiger Moth. There was no shortage of spectators, who queued up for various trial flights at 5s (25p) a trip. There were also formation flights over Edinburgh for 7s 6d (37½p). 'Rough stuff' was thrown in for 'young bloods' of all ages who got a kick out of being thrown into vertical back manoeuvres and other 'stomach shakers'. Trial flying lessons were also offered at the show, costing £1. The instructor would explain the functions

Aberdeen Airways flew DH84 G–ACAN on the short-lived Dyce–Turnhouse service in 1935. (A.J. Jackson Collection & Brooklands Museum)

Another view of Imperial Airways Armstrong Whitworth Argosy G–EBLF, this time at Turnhouse in 1930. Although Imperial did not operate a scheduled service to Turnhouse, their Argosies visited on occasions. (Museum of Flight, East Fortune)

Dalmuir-built 'Wee Bee' pictured at Turnhouse in 1930. (Museum of Flight, East Fortune)

Gypsy Moth G–ABWB took part in 'Air Days' at Maybury, Edinburgh, in the early 1930s, where 'young bloods' were given flying lessons (A.J. Jackson Collection & Brooklands Museum)

SMT (Scottish Motor Traction) DH Fox Moth G–ACEB at the SMT facility in a field at Corstorphine, 1933. (Iain Hutchison)

Hawker Harts of 603 Squadron lined up outside their hangars, RAF Turnhouse. (Museum of Flight, East Fortune)

of the aircraft controls before handing them over to the pupil mid-air. How times have changed! Unfortunately, there does not seem to be any record of how these flying lessons went.

The first site to be given any real consideration as the civil airport for Edinburgh was Gilmerton. The original selection of this site was made on 24 April 1935 after a 'London expert' had informed the Lord Provost's Committee that it would take two years to put the ground into a condition to permit its use by aircraft. The 80-acre site had been purchased by the city council at a cost of £9,000 in December 1935, but additional purchases of land were needed in order to reach a total of 116 acres. The president of the Edinburgh Chamber of Commerce, Mr A. Wallace Cowan, said in an interview with *The Scotsman* that he was very pleased the Air Ministry's approval had been received, but it was very late in the day, and he pointed out that Perth and Aberdeen both had aerodromes and that Glasgow had a daily air service to London via the Isle of Man, plus a service to Islay. There appeared to be a great deal of uncertainty on all sides regarding Gilmerton, with the Air Ministry appearing to give their approval at first then withdrawing it because of mineral deposits at the site and concern about the size and location. At a meeting of the Lord Provost's Committee of Edinburgh Town Council on 16 September 1936 it was mentioned that a letter had been received from the Air Ministry giving approval for Gilmerton and yet, barely a couple of months later, the scheme was shelved and the land which had already been purchased was sold.

3

The Norman & Dawbarn Report

In 1936 the firm of Norman & Dawbarn was invited to submit a report on all suitable sites for a new municipal airport for Edinburgh within 15 miles of the city. The '15 miles' stipulation arose from the decision not to proceed with development of a site at Gilmerton which had been favoured originally. It had first been suggested that the Gilmerton site could be developed as a small aerodrome with runways of approximately 800 yards, which would then be used to accommodate scheduled air services along with a larger main airport (to be developed at a later stage in co-operation with the county authorities) in order to serve the East Lothian region. As previously mentioned, however, on 22 July 1936, the Air Ministry stated that they could not give their permission for an airport to be developed at Gilmerton because, in their view, it was not a suitable site for a future main airport, especially as alternative locations existed. This rejection was the catalyst for Norman & Dawbarn to be appointed to look at the various sites and prepare their report with recommendations. February 1937 saw their 'Report on a Land Airport for the City of Edinburgh', which foresaw the importance of Edinburgh as the capital city and stated that 'from an aviation point of view the Eastern route from North to South is the most favourable both for weather and for terrain'. The report also predicted the importance of Highlands and Islands flights, specifically mentioning the Shetland Islands. Glasgow Airport later had the larger number of these flights, but Edinburgh has also played an important role on these routes. Just after the war (there will be more on this period in Chapter 5), the first scheduled civil flights were from Sumburgh to London through Edinburgh and Aberdeen. Flights to Lerwick and Kirkwall were added later. Norman & Dawbarn's report also speculated that there was the possibility of future traffic to Scandinavia and Northern Europe, and indeed, some seventy years later, we have seen considerable growth in Continental traffic. On the issue of long-haul traffic, the report was less prescient and, with the exception of charter flights and the scheduled US flights to New York, Newark and a planned service to Atlanta, there has been no real progress in this area. The report had stated: 'In view of the fact, that at present no really large aerodrome is available on the Western coast of Scotland, long-distance traffic for this area may also be received'. There are other reasons for the lack of long-distance traffic, and these will be examined later.

It was suggested that Edinburgh municipal airport should be of a similar size to those of Manchester, Liverpool and Birmingham, and that land should be purchased in order to facilitate this. The most important factors in any purchasing decision were to be cost and the Air Ministry 'Standard' guidelines for airports.

The report and recommendations had to fit with the Air Ministry theoretical 'Standard' requirements for airports, which were broken down into three main areas. Although the report made recommendations to fit in with these guidelines, detailed recommendations regarding airport buildings and equipment were outside its scope. Norman & Dawbarn recorded their 'appreciation of the very cordial help we have at all times received from the Town Clerk, the City Engineer and other of the city officials'. The rest of the report went on to deal with Air Ministry requirements and the examinations of the various suggested sites.

The first requirement laid down by the Air Ministry was for the landing area. In the Amendment List No.49 to Air Publication 1208 published in October 1936, it was stated that, in certain cases where additional runway lengths were available, operation of long range aircraft would be allowed with increased loading, under a special category certificate of airworthiness in which the aerodromes where such operation is permissible are mentioned specifically (Design Leaflet F1, paragraphs 9 and 10). At this time, most of the European capitals, as well as Manchester, Liverpool, Birmingham and London, already had airports, or had sites under construction. These airports were found to have runways of 1,200 to 2,000 yards in the principal directions of landing. These dimensions were set as the ministry standards. The report recommended that the area to be acquired for Edinburgh should be sufficient to provide runways of approximately 1,500 yards in the main direction of landing, allowing for avoidance of permanent obstructions by an angle of 1:15. The authors of the report considered that such provision would make the aerodrome suitable for the largest class of aircraft likely to be employed on European services at that time along with 'uninterrupted operation of all normal aircraft in all weather conditions'. The maximum gradient recommended was to be not more than 1:60, measured in the direction of landing and take off, except at the extreme edge of the landing area, where gradients of up to 1:40 would be permissible. The landing area was required to be firm enough to withstand, without permanent damage, a pressure of up to 2½ tons per sq.ft. Impact loads of up to 2 tons could be anticipated, and particular attention was drawn to drainage as well as underground pipes and culverts that should be protected from potential damage.

After laying out the standard dimensions for a municipal airport, the report then went on to discuss planning control of potential obstructions to aircraft using the airport. In 1936, neither the Air Ministry nor the Ministry of Health had offered any official guidelines regarding adequate zoning to control the erection of obstructions to aircraft. The only documentation that seemed to refer to this was Pamphlet No.55, issued by the Air Ministry, which referred in a footnote to objects likely to form obstructions. Shortly after this a diagram illustrating recommendations for zoning was published in the report of the Committee to Consider the Development of Civil Aviation in the United

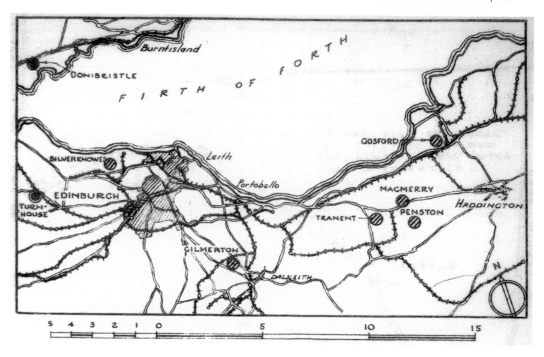

Map of potential sites for a civil airport for Edinburgh, February 1937. (Capita Norman Dawbarn)

Kingdom, under the chairmanship of Sir Henry Maybury. The report concluded their consideration of zoning by stating that they expected official regulations to be published by the Air Ministry in the 'near future'. In the meantime it was recommended that the provisions included in the recently passed private Bill for the city of Birmingham airport be taken as the basis for zoning around Class I airports, the category into which Edinburgh was expected to fall. This Bill restricted the erection of obstructions within the following parameters:

> Within 500 yards of the boundary of the airport any obstruction such that it will project above an imaginary line drawn at an angle of three degrees above the horizontal from the nearest part of the aerodrome.
>
> Between 500 and 1000 yards from the aerodrome boundary any obstruction higher than 75 feet above the nearest point of the aerodrome boundary.
>
> In prolongation of the blind landing runway, the zoning is extended by the inclusion of an approach area 500 yards long at each end of this runway upon which no buildings would be permitted; the zoning for 500 yards beyond these areas and between 500 and 1000 yards from them being similar to that around the rest of the boundary.

In the section of the report concerned with the comparisons of suggested sites, Norman & Dawbarn were instructed to examine five specific sites in terms of their suitability for the establishment of a 'Standard' airport. Initially, two sites stood out as being the most

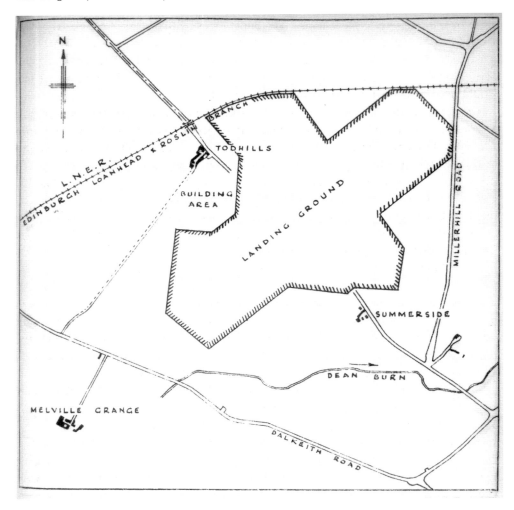

Layout of Gilmerton Site, February 1937. (Capita Norman Dawbarn)

suitable: Silverknowes and Gilmerton. Both were closely examined, but Silverknowes was rejected on account of the high cost of purchasing the land (as previously stated, cost was a determining factor). In spite of its accessibility, it was felt that construction of an aerodrome at Silverknowes would seriously interfere with other municipal schemes unrelated to the airport. At this stage the investigation was confined to Gilmerton. On this site, the high cost of the acquisition of the minerals lying below the ground made it necessary for a scheme of some kind to be prepared which would allow for access and extraction. A report prepared by the city's mining engineers (Landale, Frew & Gemmell) indicated outcrops of coal along a line crossing the north-west corner of the site as well as a fault along a line near the southern boundary. Mining would be interrupted at these two points so that the resulting subsidence (estimated at 8½ft) would only take place over an area east of the line of the break of the outcrop and north of the fault itself. To allow this, more than half of the landing area would need to be constructed north-east of the old Dalkeith Road, the road would need to be diverted, Campend Farm would need to be removed, and 'very extensive levelling and filling operations' would need to be carried out 'in the area north of the farm'. The cost of this scheme was regarded as prohibitive, and it was envisaged that the development of a smaller aerodrome which could accept scheduled air services in normal weather conditions could be developed entirely south of the old Dalkeith Road. There was an appeal to the Air Ministry to support a compulsory purchase application so that the smaller development could proceed. They responded by stating that, since the site would not be able to accommodate a 'Standard'-sized airport, they could not support a Compulsory Purchase Order. Once their reply was received, it was decided to start afresh and conduct a new and independent survey of the whole area surrounding the city of Edinburgh. Twenty-six areas were specifically examined.

It was found that there were no suitable sites located to the north-west and south-west of the city. For the first time, the possibility of a joint airport, shared with Glasgow, was considered, but the Air Ministry stated that as far as they were concerned there was no suitable site existing at that time which would serve the two cities, and the matter was dropped. However, the subject of a joint airport would surface in 1939 (with the construction of the Scottish Aviation facility at Grangemouth) and again nearly forty years later when the proposals for a new runway at Turnhouse were put forward.

To the south and east, the presence of old or active workings below the surface ruled out a number of potentially suitable sites in the Midlothian coalfields. But another site looked particularly promising. This was immediately south-east of Tranent, upon an area adjacent to the existing aerodrome at Macmerry and partially on an area south of Penston Farm near the old First World War aerodrome. Other sites more distant from the city were noted in the vicinity of the London & North Eastern Railway at Gosford Hall and also near Drem. The mining engineers Landale, Frew & Gemmell were again asked to prepare reports on these sites. Their reports indicated that the active workings below the site at Tranent rendered it unsuitable for development. They could give no absolute assurances regarding possible subsidence on the other two sites (Gosford Hall and Drem) but the view was taken that as these locations had not been worked for some considerable time, the potential danger was not too serious. However, subsequent enquiries from local sources revealed that the Penston area had seen localised subsidence of a serious nature in recent years. On one particular occasion, a carthorse was lost down a sink and, on another occasion, the collapse of an old working near the centre of the site revealed running water and required many loads of stones to fill it up. Relatives of miners who had worked in this area had indicated that there were probably a number of other shallow workings existing. After all this had been taken into account, Tranent/Penston was disregarded as a possible site. Furthermore, levels taken over the Macmerry site showed that it would not be practical to build an aerodrome there to accommodate the Air Ministry 'Standard', as local gradients exceeded 1:40. Moreover, even if an airport had been built with these excessive gradients, any future extensions would have been impossible, owing to the even steeper gradients in the surrounding areas. There was also not enough level ground for construction of airport buildings or adequate space for parking or manoeuvring of aircraft without obstructing the runways.

Fortunately, the site at Gosford had none of the shortcomings of the other sites as it was found that it could allow room for a 'Standard'-size airport to be built with plenty of room for expansion. The land was level, well-drained, and there were no old workings or minerals. Norman & Dawbarn recommended Gosford as the site most suitable for development, and it became the main subject for their report.

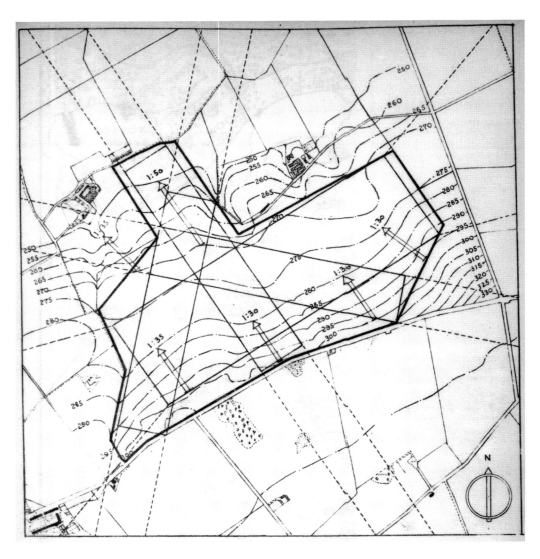

Layout of the Macmerry site, February 1937. Note the number of gradient lines. (Capita Norman Dawbarn)

In these days of the 'integrated transport system', it is interesting to see the importance given by the authors of the report to accessibility and communications at Gosford. The site lay 14 miles from the centre of Edinburgh, to the north of the Edinburgh–North Berwick Road, in the angle formed between the London & North Eastern Railway main line and the Aberlady and Gullane branch line. It was also only one mile from the railway station at Longniddry from where it was said 'the faster trains run to Edinburgh in 20 minutes'. A bus service run by the Scottish Motor Traction Company also ran past the site into Edinburgh, the journey taking 40 minutes. It was estimated that the car journey from Gosford to Princes Street would take 30 minutes, due to 'a large proportion of the distance being subject to the 30mph restriction'.

Overall the report favoured the Gosford site as the most suitable for Edinburgh's municipal airport. The report gave a preliminary and a master plan for the 278-acre landing site. The preliminary plan, costing £7,916, allowed for four runways between 850 and 1,060 yards whilst the master scheme, costing £28,735, allowed for four runways between 1,000 yards and 1,500 yards. The report did not take into account the cost, design or layout of any aerodrome buildings or airfield lighting, airport equipment or removal of obstructions such as trees. However, despite Gosford's apparent suitability, the town clerk of Edinburgh Corporation received a letter dated 15 June 1938 from the Air Ministry which stated that they felt Macmerry would be a good location for a 'Standard Aerodrome' (in spite of the excessive gradients mentioned in the Norman & Dawbarn report). This letter went on to state that arrangements had been made for the RAF to have a station at Drem and that, on account of this, any proposed aerodrome at Gosford would have to be ruled out owing to its close proximity. Gosford was duly ruled out on 22 June 1938. Macmerry was brought up again at a meeting of the Lord Provost's Committee on 7 September 1938, when the town clerk submitted correspondence with the Air Ministry regarding Macmerry. The correspondence stated that the ministry required a further 68 acres in addition to its current 107.5 acres for the RAF Volunteer Reserve. It was felt that in order to accommodate a 'Standard' aerodrome, a total of 650 acres would be needed in addition to planning controls on erections and any obstructions in the surrounding areas. At the end of this committee meeting, it was decided to contact the Scottish Aviation Co. (who leased Macmerry) for negotiations.

Despite the time, trouble and expense spent on the report, along with extensive discussions about the sites, the Second World War was fast approaching, and such matters tended to be put to one side. Furthermore, not everyone was totally in favour of a new airport. Although not a direct opponent of the civil airport for Edinburgh, City Treasurer Sir William Y. Darling MP said pointedly to the town council on 21 April 1938 that, 'No airport can be an economic proposition for the city'. The town council had gone far and wide to find justification for the airport enterprise he said, but they could not find that justification. 'Have we any right to ask the citizens of Edinburgh who do not fly to pay rates for the support of this means of travel?', he asked. He followed this up with a lengthy article in *The Scotsman* on 5 May 1938, headed, 'An airport for Edinburgh – is it the function of the Municipality?' He fully agreed on the desirability of an airport but felt very strongly that it should be funded by the government or private enterprise.

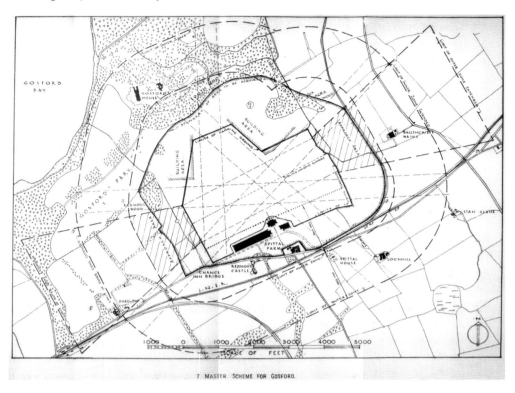

7. MASTER SCHEME FOR GOSFORD.

The master scheme for Gosford, February 1937. This site was recommended by Norman & Dawbarn as being the most suitable for a future Edinburgh Airport. (Capita Norman Dawbarn)

He went on to criticise the delays in finding a suitable site for an airport, mentioning Gilmerton, Silverknowes and Macmerry, but he had the foresight to say a suitable site already existed at Turnhouse, and that airfields at Drem and East Fortune were going to limit any future choices in selecting a suitable site. He felt that the government was taking the 'easy way out' by calling on municipalities to provide aerodromes. There were none in 1928, but there were thirty-three licensed municipal aerodromes ten years later. He mentioned the recently published Maybury report on the establishment of aerodromes, which had stated that the finances of a municipal airport would be unsatisfactory and receipts would be negligible for many years to come. He went on to mention the 738 municipal aerodromes in the USA, eighty-four of which were taken as a sample. Taking into account depreciation and payment of interest and principal on the bonds issued for airport loans, not a single one of the sample of eighty-four would show a profit. He felt that the whole subject of airport building and running should be approached in a more controlled manner. He mentioned the electricity industry, in which millions of pounds had been spent uneconomically before the Central Electricity Board was set up, followed by millions more in making the service national. Sir William Young Darling MP (as he was to become) was later to act as Honorary Air Commodore to 603 Squadron from 1943 to 1951.

Of course, no one could have foreseen the future growth of air travel or understood fully the need for air services, but the article is indicative of the difficulties facing the establishment of an airport in Edinburgh at the time.

The next mention of a joint airport for Glasgow and Edinburgh was made by Mr F.C.R. Jaques, the managing director of North Eastern Airways Ltd in a letter to the *Edinburgh Evening News* on 9 April 1938. It was a concept that would raise its head on more than one occasion in decades to come. In a letter to *The Scotsman* the previous September Jaques had stated that North Eastern Airways had been compelled to avoid Edinburgh altogether due to the lack of suitable facilities, but were in a position to serve Macmerry as it had been expanded. Their timetable stipulated Edinburgh as a 'request stop', and the stop would only be made weather and other conditions permitting. He also pointed out that no wireless facilities existed at Macmerry. In this letter of 27 September 1937, Mr Jaques added: 'excuse our going into so much detail, but we do not wish to do the air service harm by creating a wrong impression in the beginning as to what we are offering your city in the way of an air service'.

Macmerry itself was ruled out as a civil airport for Edinburgh at a meeting of the Lord Provost's Committee on 26 January 1939. This was decided after a meeting with Scottish Aviation Ltd (who still held the lease on the land). The committee meeting decided that the additional levelling costs which would be required would be prohibitive and it was decided to consider other options.

One of these options was the Scottish Aviation Facility at Grangemouth. A letter was sent to Edinburgh Corporation on 13 February 1939 stating that they were preparing a facility and aerodrome at Grangemouth and suggested this could serve as a Central Scotland Airport serving both Edinburgh and Glasgow. At the Lord Provost's Committee meeting on the 15 February 1939 the Lord Provost, Bailie Sawers and Treasurer Darling were deputed to meet with Scottish Aviation to discuss the matter. Whether this took place is not mentioned, as any future references (during the war) in Edinburgh Corporation's minutes with regard to an Edinburgh airport mention only Turnhouse. There is a mention at a Lord Provost's Committee meeting on 16 January 1947 of a 'lack of heavy workers' in the preparation of Turnhouse for civil flights. Will Darling was present at the actual official opening of Grangemouth aerodrome by Lord Trenchard. The Second World War was to put Edinburgh's civil airport on hold.

The Grangemouth facility opened in July 1939 and Scottish Aviation later moved the facility to Prestwick. One of the pioneers of Scottish Aviation, David F. McIntyre, had formed a company called Night Air Transport Limited registered at 3 Glenfinlas Street, Edinburgh. The aim had been to use three ex-KLM Fokker airliners (two F22s and an F36) for carrying mail and cargo from Grangemouth to London but unfortunately the war intervened. It would have been interesting to see if Grangemouth would have grown as an airport serving both Edinburgh and Glasgow had the war not taken place.

In February 1938 Squadron Leader John W. Gillan, of 111 Squadron, flying a Hurricane, set a new speed record between Northolt and Turnhouse of 48 minutes for the 327 miles journey at an average speed of 408.75mph. Sadly, Wing Commander Gillan (as he became later, also winning the DFC and AFC) was later killed in action over the English Channel on 29 August 1941.

Grangemouth Airport on its opening day, July 1939. KLM DC3 PH–ASR in the foreground. Grangemouth was proposed as a Central Scotland Airport by its owners Scottish Aviation. (Dougal McIntyre)

As the Second World War approached, Turnhouse started to get busier with fighter and transport aircraft (83 Bombing Squadron had re-formed there in August 1936 with Hawker Hinds before moving to RAF Scampton in March 1938) and it was decided to replace the grass runways.

The original three hardened runways were laid down in 1939 and completed by the end of that year. They were 13/31 (3,900ft), 08/26 (3,300ft) and 04/22 (2,100ft). Although slightly shorter than 13/31, 08/26 was most frequently used as it was aligned into the prevailing wind. 04/22 was provided for use in the most south-westerly gales. In later years, the 13/31 was strengthened and lengthened to its current 6,000ft. However, frequent diversions and cancellations due to crosswinds on the runway resulted in demands for a new runway to be built. The Second World War and the laying down of hardened runways was really the impetus needed to give Edinburgh the basis for its future civil airport.

4

The Second World War

On 27 October 1938, 603 Squadron was transferred to Fighter Command as part of 12 (Fighter) Group, later coming under the control of 13 Group. Also in 1938 it won the Esher Trophy for the best all-round flying performance by an auxiliary squadron. The trophy, a bronze figure of Perseus, was presented to the squadron by the late Viscount Esher. The squadron were to win the trophy again in 1950. On 23 August 1939, the squadron was officially integrated into the RAF. There was a selection of training aircraft used by 603 towards the end of the 1930s. The Lynx Avro 504N aircraft were replaced in 1937 by the Avro Tutor, and later the DH Tiger Moth II, Miles Magister I and the mainstay of pilot training, the North American Harvard. Two DH Moth 60Ms had also been used for training from 1931 to 1938.

Having been disbanded in Ireland in February 1920, No.141 Squadron re-formed at Turnhouse on 4 October 1939, receiving some Gloster Gladiators and later Bristol Blenheims. These two types formed the training equipment of the unit until they were equipped with Boulton Paul Defiants in April 1940 becoming operational on this type on 3 June 1940 and flying its first operational patrol on the 29 June 1940. The squadron moved south to West Malling on 12 July 1940 but was no match for the German fighters, mainly due to the fact that the Defiant had no guns facing forward. It was withdrawn for re-training as a night fighter unit and spent the early part of September 1940 back at Turnhouse.

A very memorable day for 603 Squadron was 16 October 1939, when a Spitfire from the squadron (operating from RAF Turnhouse) was responsible for the first downing of a German aircraft over Britain in the Second World War (only six weeks into the conflict). The squadron beat its friendly rivals – 602 City of Glasgow Squadron – by 15 minutes.

On that morning the commander of Luftwaffe KG/30, Hauptmann Helmut Pohle, led four groups, each comprising three Junkers Ju 88s, across the North Sea from their base at Sylt on a daylight raid to Scotland. Its targets were Royal Navy ships in the Firth of Forth. At a high level meeting in Berlin with the head of the Luftwaffe, Pohle had been told by Hermann Goering that the vessels making things difficult were HMS *Renown*, HMS *Repulse* and HMS *Hood*, along with the aircraft-carriers. Pohle's orders were to attack the *Hood* only at sea and not in dock. The aircraft crossed the British mainland at

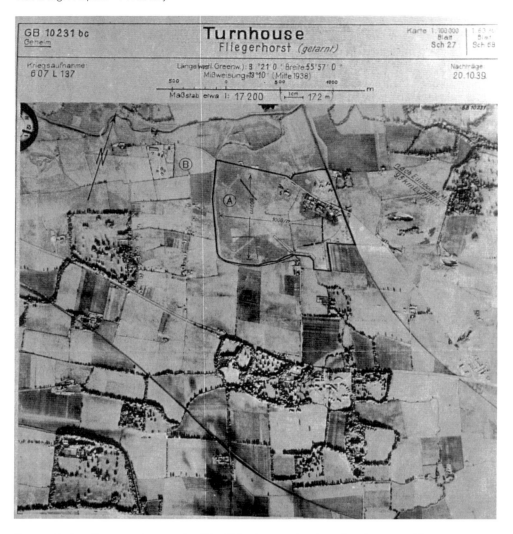

German Luftwaffe target photograph of RAF Turnhouse taken just after the start of the war on 20 October 1939 (Sqdn Ldr Bruce Blanche Collection, via 603 Squadron Association. Picture reproduced by permission of Bundesarchiv-Bildarchiv, Koblenz – Bundesrepublik, Deutschland)

Berwick and made their way towards the Firth of Forth. There were numerous sightings of unidentified aircraft – one searchlight crew claimed to have spotted six Henschels, but these turned out to be Sea Skuas from RNAS Donibristle. Three Spitfires of Blue section 602 Squadron had already taken off from Drem on patrol, and were directed to intercept enemy aircraft.

The Royal Navy vessels in the Firth of Forth were HMS *Edinburgh* and HMS *Southampton* with HMS *Mohawk*, HMS *Jervis* and the aircraft-carrier HMS *Furious*. Once the attack started, 603's Yellow section was scrambled to intercept the bombers, Red section having taken off 5 minutes before and vectored towards Drem. Yellow section caught up with three of the Ju 88s over Colinton and attacked once clear of the city. One Ju 88 was hit and swung north, flying over Roslin and Laighill Farm. Red section took up the attack after intercepting over Carberry Hill, whilst the two from Yellow section returned to re-arm. The Ju 88 crashed into the sea near Port Seton with one of the crew already dead and the other three to become prisoners. Flt Lt Pat Gifford, in his Spitfire, *Stickleback*, claimed the first 'kill' of the war. The other Ju 88 shot down was flown by the commander of the group, Helmut Pohle. He was attacked by two Spitfires of Blue section 602 Squadron, flown by George Pinkerton and Archie McKellar who had taken up position over Tranent. Unable to shake off his attackers, and with two crew already dead and one wounded, Pohle's Ju 88 crashed into the sea. The wounded crew member later died and Pohle was the only survivor. In all there were three initial waves of attacks on the two cruisers but, despite a few casualties, nobody was seriously injured on these

Construction of airfield defences, September 1939. (David Ross)

'A' Flight, 603 Squadron, 16 October 1939. (David Ross)

vessels. The 2.30 p.m. train from Edinburgh to Dunfermline had rumbled over the Forth Rail Bridge while the attack was in progress as no air-raid warning had sounded up to that point.

One group of Ju 88s which had separated from the others came in to attack 30 minutes after the initial attack led by Pohle. Two 500kg bombs landed within 50ft of the destroyer HMS *Mohawk*, resulting in the deaths of two officers and thirteen ratings. The captain (Commander Richard Jolly) was to die later from shrapnel wounds. Two of the Ju 88s started to make their escape by flying over RAF Turnhouse, while the other flew over Turnhouse golf course. A Spitfire from 603 Squadron chased one of the Ju 88s at 300ft over the rooftops of Edinburgh, flying over Raeburn Place and Abercrombie Place. Jim 'Black' Morton, in another Spitfire, caught up with a Junkers over Portobello, and opened fire, along with Robbie Robertson who had trailed the Ju 88 over Edinburgh. Two bullets went into the home of the Lord Provost Sir Henry Steel at 10 Hamilton Drive, and the masonry was pitted. Another spent bullet was found on a bed at 7 Coillesdene Crescent by resident Mr H. Robertson. Joe McLuskie was hit by one of the bullets as he held a ladder for painter Frank Flynn at 45 Abercorn Terrace. He was rushed to Leith Hospital where the bullet was removed from his stomach. Houses in Morton Street and Joppa Road, Portobello, were also damaged.

The actions of that day were a great morale boost to the squadron and Robbie Robertson won a DFC for his action that day and for his expertise as a gunnery instructor. Pat Gifford of 603 Squadron was also awarded a DFC, in part for his contribution on the 16 October. Years later it was discovered that, in addition to the two Ju 88s shot down, another which was badly hit had crashed miles off course near Breda in Holland, killing the crew.

On 22 October, barely a week after the action with the Ju 88s, Red section intercepted a Heinkel 111 off St Abbs Head and shot it down, the aircraft ditching in the sea. Another Heinkel 111 was shot down by three Spitfires of 603's Red section along with Spitfires from 602 Squadron. The Heinkel came down just east of the village of Humbie near Kidlaw, 6 miles south of Haddington, thus becoming the first German aircraft to be shot down over land (the previous aircraft had gone into the sea). The machine gun from this particular aircraft is now displayed in the National War Museum of Scotland.

For the rest of 1939 until it was transferred to Prestwick on 16 December, 603 Squadron defended Scottish ports and shipping. After a short stay at Drem, 603 Squadron moved back to Turnhouse on 5 May 1940 (with detachments at Montrose and Dyce) and were given their squadron badge on 2 June 1940, with the motto 'Gin Ye Daur' ('If You Dare'). The Maybury Roadhouse and the D'Guise nightclub in the Caledonian Hotel were favoured watering holes for members of the squadron. The squadron moved to Hornchurch on 28 August 1940, becoming the highest scoring squadron with 58½ 'kills'. The squadron then moved to Drem and back to Turnhouse on 28 February 1941, before transferring again to Hornchurch in May of that year.

In the early part of the war (pre-1942), the Operations Controller at Turnhouse was future Air Vice-Marshall Sandy Johnstone DFC who had previously commanded 602 (City of Glasgow) Squadron at the age of twenty-four. His first 'kill' was a Heinkel 111,

Crashed Luftwaffe Heinkel 111. This was the first enemy warplane to be shot down on British soil (the earlier Ju 88s ended up in the sea) by Spitfires of 603 and 602 Squadrons. Known as the 'Humbie Heinkel', it came down east of Humbie near Kidlaw on 22 October 1939. A machine gun from this aircraft is on display in the museum at Edinburgh Castle, and the flying suit of the observer and first officer are in the archive and can be viewed on request. (Museum of Flight, East Fortune)

10 miles east of Dunbar. Another pilot who was to make a great impression joined 603 Squadron in 1941. This was Wilfred Duncan-Smith, who was to finish the war with a distinguished flying record. He was later to command 603 Squadron in the post-war years. He was the father of the former Conservative Party leader Iain Duncan-Smith. Iain was born at the Simpson Memorial Hospital in Edinburgh and the first year of his life was actually spent living at Aeroville Lodge (used as the Commanding Officers Quarters) at Turnhouse. He has said that he always feels as though he has arrived home when he lands at Edinburgh, and he is one of the few people who can say it really *was* home!

RAF Turnhouse was a key station during the Battle of Britain and it was a Sector Airfield of 13 Group, which had its administrative HQ at RAF Newcastle. I will explain briefly its part in the structure. The defence of the UK was split into four groups; under the group Headquarters were Sector Airfields, under them came Fighter Airfields and, built into this, were Chain Home Stations (for early warning of raids) and Chain Home Low Stations (to give low-level raid cover). Seven squadrons operated from Turnhouse during the course of the battle – 603 Sqdn from 5 May 1940, 141 Sqdn from 28 June 1940, 253 Sqdn from 21 July 1940, 65 Sqdn from 28 August 1940, 141 Sqdn from 30 August 1940, 1 Sqdn from 14 September 1940 and finally 607 Sqdn from 10 October 1940. Hurricanes from 3 Squadron were present in September and October 1940. RAF Turnhouse was bombed for the first time on 26 June 1940. Two Spitfire Squadrons (Nos 122 and 123) were re-formed in May 1941. On 26 June 1941, Squadron 122 moved to Ouston.

On 20 October 1940 General De Gaulle approved the establishment of the Free French No.340 Squadron named 'Ile de France' composed of two flights named 'Paris' and 'Versailles'. This was formed at Turnhouse on 7 November 1941 with Spitfire MkIIs. The Squadron became operational on 29 November 1941 and flew defensive patrols from Turnhouse before moving to Redhill in April 1942. The squadron was commanded by a British officer (Squadron Leader Loft) and it had a strong contingent of Tahitians. Half of the mechanics for the squadron were also British. General De Gaulle visited the squadron at Turnhouse on 12 February 1942 where he was presented with the Cross of Lorraine which had been made by members of 340 Squadron. The squadron returned for brief periods in March and April 1943 and in February 1945. Another Squadron, No.341 was formed from Free French personnel at Turnhouse on the 15 January 1943 with Spitfires. They moved to Biggin Hill in March 1943.

Personnel from 81 Squadron assembled at Turnhouse in December 1941 to work up on Spitfires. A detachment was based at Ouston, and eventually the whole squadron moved there in April 1942. No.4 Delivery Flight was based at Turnhouse from 8 January 1942 to ferry fighter aircraft within 11 Group.

On 10 April 1942, 242 Squadron re-formed, and it too moved to Ouston in May of that year. The squadron consisted of Canadians in the RAF, and was known as 242 (Canadian) Squadron. The Fleet Air Arm (FAA) 801 Squadron was present at Turnhouse in early 1942 with Sea Hurricanes. The HQ of 289 Squadron moved from Kirknewton to Turnhouse after 20 May 1942, and stayed until 7 May 1945. This squadron was equipped with Hurricanes, Oxfords and Defiants but was not a front-line squadron.

Despite the hardships imposed by war conditions, the subject of a civil airport for the city of Edinburgh was never too far from the minds of the Lord Provost's Committee. At a meeting of the committee on 25 November 1942, Councillor Sawers submitted a

Avro 19 Anson, Turnhouse 1943. Although not the best-known aircraft of the war, 11,000 were produced after its first flight in 1935. (Squadron Leader Bruce Blanche Collection)

WAAFS working on a Miles Master at Turnhouse in 1944. (Museum of Flight, East Fortune)

motion to review the question of the necessity for a civil aerodrome within a reasonable distance from the centre of the city. At the same meeting a motion was put forward 'to consider the formation of an invasion committee'.

In addition to 801 Squadron, other FAA (Fleet Air Arm) units were often attached to Turnhouse, especially when disembarked from aircraft-carriers in the Firth of Forth. From February 1942 to July 1943, Squadron Nos 882, 884 and 808 were all present at some stage, being equipped with Martlets, Fulmars and Seafires respectively. No.886 FAA Squadron was attached to 13 Group and spent most of 1943 at Turnhouse flying Seafires and Spitfires. No.882 had also been attached to 13 Group in February/March 1942, as had 884 for brief periods. Squadron No.895 of the FAA disbanded at Turnhouse in June 1943 to form 816 and 842 FAA Squadrons. Nos 232 and 234 were also present briefly in 1942 before both squadrons were transferred overseas.

No.63 Tactical Reconnaissance Squadron arrived in July 1943 with Mustangs to participate in training exercises, before moving to Thruxton in November 1943. The squadron returned in January 1944 to re-equip with Hurricanes, and trained for bombardment spotting with the Royal Navy whilst awaiting attachment to the D-Day landing forces. No.268 Squadron was posted to Turnhouse from November 1943 to January 1944 with Mustangs.

At a special sub-committee meeting (of the Lord Provost's Committee) on civil aerodromes on 19 January 1944, it was resolved to recommend that the Air Ministry should be advised that Edinburgh Corporation were still interested in the provision of civil air services in the region and in particular that no action would be taken by the Ministry which may prejudice the use of Turnhouse without the knowledge of the Corporation. The response of the Air Ministry in February 1944 was that no decisions had been made regarding civil air transport after the war but that they had taken note of the Corporation's interest in Turnhouse. In the meantime, Turnhouse continued as an active military base, with 290 Squadron (target towing) arriving in August 1944 from Long Kesh and leaving in January 1945. No.329 Squadron was at Turnhouse briefly with Spitfires in March 1945 before going on to Skeabrae. June 1945 saw the arrival of 164 Squadron to re-equip with Spitfires. They left in November 1945 but returned

Spitfire F22s at Turnhouse after the war. (David Ross)

for a few months in January 1946. This squadron consisted mainly of Argentinians, and was therefore known as the 'Argentine-British Squadron'. Over 600 Argentinians volunteered to fight with the British and Canadian Air Forces during the war, and the shield of 164 bore the sun of the Argentine flag and the motto 'Determined We Fly' (Firmes Volamos).

Turnhouse also played host to large numbers of American aircraft particularly towards the end of the war, as Edinburgh was a favoured destination for 'rest and recreation'. No.303 (Polish) Squadron took up residence at Turnhouse with Mustang MkIVs from 28 November 1945 until their transfer to Wick on 4 January 1946. This squadron was named 'Kosciuszko' after the Polish American hero Tadeiusz Kosciuszko and was considered the most effective of the Polish squadrons, having achieved the highest number of 'kills' of all sixty-six squadrons which took part in the Battle of Britain. They destroyed nearly forty enemy aircraft. For this achievement, pilots of 303 were invited to take part in the London victory parade in 1946. They refused, however, as no other elements of the Polish forces had been invited. Their last operational sortie on the 23 April 1945 was to escort RAF Lancasters on a bombing raid on Hitler's Berchtesgaden.

On 10 April 1945 elements of No.88 Group of the Allied Expeditionary Force were established at Turnhouse, involving Nos 330, 333 and 334 (all general reconnaissance squadrons) of the Royal Norwegian Air Force.

After a lengthy absence, 603 Squadron returned to Turnhouse for a brief period in April/May and again in July 1945, with the squadron being disbanded on 15 August 1945. After the rigours and trials of war, the pilots of 603 now had to face the monotony of peace. It was reported that the Forth Rail Bridge was used by some Spitfire pilots to test their skills by flying loops around the narrow sections of the bridge.

In May 1945 Spitfires from 603 at Turnhouse escorted three Junkers Ju 52s into Drem. The Luftwaffe transports had brought in representatives of the three German services in Norway to offer the surrender of troops there and make arrangements for the end of the occupation.

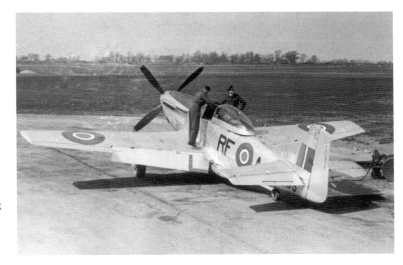

303 (Polish) Squadron Mustang IV. (Via Wilhelm Ratuszynski/ J.B. Cynk)

303 (Polish) Squadron Mustang IV KH770. (Via Wilhelm Ratuszynski/ J.B. Cynk)

5
Post-war

On 10 May 1946, 603 Squadron was re-formed at Turnhouse and were to be equipped with nine Spitfire MkXVIEs. The training flight was to receive four Spitfire MkXVIEs and two Harvard IIBs. On 1 October 1946, operational control of Turnhouse was transferred from Fighter to Reserve Command. Control of Turnhouse then passed from the RAF to the MTCA (Ministry of Transport & Civil Aviation) on 19 May 1947. There were no customs facilities at Turnhouse during 1946, but these were eventually provided from 19 May 1947.

The Empire Air Day event was restarted in May 1947, attracting 8,000 visitors. These were popular with the public, attracting pre-war crowds of up to 17,500. The 'At Home' Days and Battle of Britain Day (BoB Day was held in September of each year at various RAF stations, and continues to this day) were also very popular with the public. Edinburgh became the first Scottish city to raise a squadron of the Royal Auxiliary Air Force Regiment and an air defence unit. On the 23 May 1947, 2603 (City of Edinburgh) Light Anti-Aircraft Regiment squadron was formed, based at RAF Turnhouse. Its primary role was airfield defence, and it was equipped with 40mm Bofors anti-aircraft guns. No.2603 was affiliated to 603 Squadron and shared the town HQ at Learmonth Terrace. It was to be disbanded on 10 March 1957, along with the other Light AA Regiment squadrons.

The 25 November 1947 was to see an RAF Gloster Meteor arrive from the Central Flying Establishment at RAF West Raynham. Piloted by twenty-eight-year-old Squadron Leader James Lomas DFC, the Meteor took off from Turnhouse and travelled to Bovingdon in Hertfordshire, a distance of 313.1 miles which was covered in 30 minutes and 25 seconds, at an average speed of 617.6mph. The purpose of the flight was to compare the times with the record set by the Hawker Hurricane flown by John Gillan in 1938 (Bovingdon is not far from Northolt). This was a creditable performance when set against the records set by later aircraft like the Hunter and Phantom in years to come. The world speed record at the time of the Meteor's flight was held by a US Navy Douglas Skystreak at 650.6mph. The Skystreak had broken the record set by a Meteor earlier in 1947.

In March 1948 3603 (City of Edinburgh) Air Defence Unit was formed at RAF Turnhouse, sharing a hut with 2603 LAA squadron. In May 1948 the unit moved to the newly opened Sector Operations Centre of 12 Fighter Group RAF at Barnton Quarry. Unit 3603 was later re-designated Fighter Control Unit (FCU). The unit's town headquarters were opened in 1953 at 16 Royal Terrace. When 603 Squadron was disbanded on 10 March 1957, the FCU moved their town headquarters to 25 Learmonth Terrace until they too were disbanded on 1 November 1959.

As part of an RAF recruitment drive, February 1949 saw the largest flying display over the skies of Edinburgh since before the war. Six Gloster Meteors, five Avro Lincoln bombers (from RAF Binbrook), twenty Supermarine Spitfires and five DH Vampires all flew over the city, in addition to a ground procession along Princes Street and demonstrations of equipment by various units at the Mound car park. The Battle of Britain 'At Home' day on 26 June 1949 proved popular with the public, attracting over 30,000 visitors. Around 25,000 were present for the 1950 'At Home' day.

All the early scheduled operations from Turnhouse after the Second World War and into the 1950s were operated by BEA. Some of the first flights were operated with Junkers Ju 52s (these ex-Luftwaffe transport aircraft were part of a batch of 100 requisitioned by the Allies at the end of the war; a number were reconditioned by Short Bros in Belfast, given civil registrations G–AHOC to G–AHOL and then used by BEA). BEA named these aircraft 'Jupiters'. In the early 1950s BEA would follow this practice of giving all their types of aircraft a class name. The Ju 52s/Jupiters had been acquired in turn from Railway Air Services and Scottish Airways. BEA spent a large sum of money for the time (£12,500) modifying and refurbishing each aircraft. They were employed on the Sumburgh–Aberdeen–Turnhouse–Northolt route, six days a week from 19 May 1947 until 31 August 1947 when BEA withdrew this particular aircraft from service. The withdrawal of the Jupiters was mainly due to a chronic shortage of useable spares and a lack of ground power units at Scottish airfields (only Glasgow and Turnhouse had them) which meant having to leave one engine running when no unit was available. DC3s were then used by BEA on this route (the fare for the 2½-hour journey from London to Edinburgh being exactly £8 single and £11 return in 1948/49), which continued to be operated six days a week, and was discontinued during the winter of 1947/48 to be reinstated in the spring of 1948. This left Edinburgh without an air link to London from October 1947 to March 1948 and led to many complaints from the authorities and business community in Edinburgh. Services were resumed on 1 April 1948 when a BEA Pionair (Pionair was the class name given to the DC3s modified and operated by BEA) landed from Renfrew on its way to Northolt. The separate Northolt–Turnhouse–Aberdeen–Shetland/Orkney route was discontinued from 18 April 1948. The Ju 52 Jupiters were broken up at Warrington/Castle Bromwich in 1948.

The Scottish Manager of KLM, Mr W. Ten Hoven, stated on 8 February 1948 that KLM were looking at the possibility of an Amsterdam–Turnhouse service. This was somewhat ironic considering that the national airline BEA had stopped services from London at this time. The plan was to start with a passenger service using DC3s and then expand the service to transport fruit, early vegetables and flowers from Amsterdam to Edinburgh. The service however did not proceed due to operational and technical considerations.

In 1948, 7,000 passengers were recorded, although Turnhouse did not officially open as a civil airport until 1 April 1949. Lord Douglas of Kirtleside (the chairman of BEA) was at Northolt to greet the arrival of the reopened service from Edinburgh which arrived just after 11.00 a.m. on 1 April 1949, and also to host a lunch for various dignitaries connected with the service. He mentioned that the initial services from Edinburgh the previous year had been operating at a capacity as low as 20 per cent but that by October the figure had risen to 65 per cent soon after the fares had been lowered to £11 return. He pointed out that this was lower than the first-class return railway fares if one included sleepers. The service had been timed so that people could travel to London, complete their business and return the same day, or alternatively to leave Edinburgh in the morning and arrive in almost any one of the European capitals by connecting within the same day. He also looked beyond the current service operated by DC3s and said that Edinburgh would probably need longer runways to accommodate the aircraft which would replace the current generation. One of the dignitaries on the flight from Edinburgh was Mr J. Murray Watson, editor of the *Scotsman*, who stated that people wanted the cheaper fare and a regular service. A spokesman for BEA said later the same day that bookings for Easter of that year were already up to 50 per cent and that the service could be stepped up for the Festival if the demand was there.

Even after the war there were still problems to be overcome in firmly establishing the airport. There were delays in the provision of equipment for 'year round' use, and services were suspended or curtailed. However, for once the airport had a vigorous champion in Lord Provost Sir Andrew Murray, who refused to accept official excuses for delays and problems. He went to London and told the heads of BEA what the people of Edinburgh wanted. In February 1951, when the government tried to side-track Turnhouse as a civil airport once again, Sir Andrew said, 'On every big issue now the Scottish people have to be vocal to get something done. It is no use going through the usual channels of committees. The only way now is to rise up in wrath and let them see that we are not going to be trifled with'. Eventually the pressure exerted by Sir Andrew and the business community forced a restoration and improvement of services.

6
The 1950s and 1960s

For a short period at the end of 1950, 603 Squadron was commanded by Squadron Leader Joe Holmes. Joe went on to more senior postings in the RAF but is remembered and credited with being the person who shot up Field Marshall Erwin Rommel (The Desert Fox) when he was touring German front-line positions in Normandy in July 1944. Cannon fire from a 266 Squadron Hawker Typhoon 1B caused Rommel to be hit by broken glass. A blow on the left temple and cheek bone fractured his skull and he was taken to hospital unconscious. Research showed that the attacking aircraft was almost certainly the one flown by Joe Holmes.

An unusual and innovative air service was started on 7 July 1950 operated by Aquila Airways using Hythe Class flying boats, the proving flight to Edinburgh being flown by Captain Andrew Evans on June 2 1950. Aquila's fleet consisted solely of flying boats. The Southampton to Glasgow and Edinburgh service was operated to Greenock for Glasgow and Leith Marine Airport (which had been licensed by the Ministry of Civil Aviation) for Edinburgh. The Leith mooring point was just off Albert Dock head with passengers taken to and from the aircraft by launch. The service was aimed at ships' passengers in Southampton and Scotland, holidaymakers to and from Scotland and air cargo. The single fare was £9 with the return fare costing £16 4s. The journey from Southampton to Edinburgh took 2 hours. Aquila Airways was one of the first independent airlines to operate scheduled flights after the war and this was due to its close relationship with BEA (British scheduled routes had been nationalised by the government in August 1946). Sadly, the services to Edinburgh and Glasgow stopped almost as soon as they had started due to heavy losses on the routes. Aquila themselves ceased trading in 1958 despite showing a £90,000 profit in 1957 and despite providing aircraft for the Berlin Airlift using Lake Havel, and operating a previously profitable service to Madeira from Southampton via Lisbon. Aquila Airways had also used their flying boats for profitable charter work. However, the airline faced difficulties in obtaining spare parts for its flying boats and faced stiff competition from land-based airlines like Dan Air.

From 15–23 August 1950 during the period of the Edinburgh Festival, BEA introduced a prototype Viscount, G–AHRF, on flights from Northolt direct to Edinburgh. Control of Turnhouse was to revert back to the RAF in 1952, becoming a 'Joint User' aerodrome,

A BEA Douglas DC3 Pionair landing at Turnhouse. (Gordon Pearson)

Vickers Viking VL247 of the King's Flight visiting Turnhouse in 1950. Of the 163 Vikings built, four were assigned to the King's Flight. The King's Flight officially became the Queen's Flight on 1 August 1952 after the death of King George VI in February of that year. (Gordon Pearson)

before finally being handed back to civilian control on 1 July 1960 when the Ministry of Civil Aviation took over.

With the introduction of jet aircraft to the Royal Auxiliary Air Force a runway extension was necessary, and it was decided to extend 13/31 to the south-east to a total length of 6000ft. This extension work started on the 23 April 1951 and was completed in the late summer of 1952. ORPS (Operational Readiness Platforms) were also provided at each end of 13/31 as part of the work carried out. These ORPS have been used in

Short Solent G–ANYI of Aquila Airways. Aquila Airways operated a mixed fleet of Short Sunderlands and Solents. The first flight from Southampton to Leith was undertaken by a Sunderland (A.J. Jackson Collection & Brooklands Museum)

DH89 Rapide G–AKRS. This aircraft is now in the Israeli Defence Force museum in Israel. (Gordon Pearson)

later years as additional parking areas at busy times (the shorter 08/26 runway has also been used for additional parking for diversions from other airports and charter aircraft for international rugby matches).

May 1951 saw 603 Squadron begin to receive new Vampire FB.5s. At around this time, the squadron returned to Turnhouse from RAF Leuchars, where they had been temporarily based while the runway extension was constructed. These new Vampires took part in the 1952 Battle of Britain air display in September at Turnhouse. The last

603 Squadron DH Vampire WR 156, Turnhouse 1951. This aircraft was built at Chester. (Gordon Pearson)

Gloster Meteor taxiing on to main apron. (Robert Whitton)

603 Spitfires flew on 1 July 1951 when a formation of ten MkF22 Spitfires flew over Edinburgh from east to west along Princes Street. Most definitely this was the end of a proud era. The Vampires (as well as two Meteor 7s) remained at Turnhouse until 1957.

From 1950–1953 a daily Monday to Saturday return service was operated from Northolt to Edinburgh–Aberdeen–Kirkwall–Lerwick by BEA Pionairs. In Spring 1952 a DC3 Pionair service was operated from Kirkwall to Aberdeen–Turnhouse–Manchester. BEA also inaugurated a service to Birmingham from Turnhouse on 1 April 1953, with some flights routed via Manchester.

The first scheduled international flight was operated by Aer Lingus which started flights to Dublin on 22 April 1952 using DC3s. The first service was operated by EI–ACE. The incoming flight from Dublin brought representatives of the Irish government, the city of Dublin and Aer Lingus (including Mr Frank Aiken the Irish Minister for External Affairs and the Lord Mayor of Dublin). It was met by the Lord Provost of Edinburgh,

Vampire NF.10s and Hunter F.6s, c.1950s. (Gordon Pearson)

Gloster Meteor VW457 T.7 151/43 Squadron, 20 September 1958. (Gordon Pearson)

DH Mosquito TT35 VR806, 20 September 1958. Built as a model B.35 at Christchurch, it was converted to a TT.35 at Sywell, serving with 5 Civilian Anti-Aircraft Co-operation Unit before being struck off charge on 16 December 1959. (Gordon Pearson)

Mr James Miller and the Lady Provost Mrs Miller along with other dignitaries. The Edinburgh City Police Pipe Band played 'The Green Hills of Tyrone' as a welcome. With a 90-minute flying time, there were three return flights a week with a daily service in the summer months. The service proved to be popular, carrying approximately 5,000 passengers in its first year.

A T2 hangar was erected in 1952 to house the Vampires of 603 Squadron. When 603 disbanded in March 1957, the hangar was used temporarily by the Javelins of 151 Squadron from June 1957 until their return to RAF Leuchars in October/November of that year. While 151 Squadron was at Turnhouse, they were in the process of replacing their Vampires with Javelin FAW.5s and most of the deliveries of the new Javelins were made direct to 151 at Turnhouse. Research has shown that the T2 hangar was originally located at RAF Turnberry and was subsequently dismantled, transported and reassembled at Turnhouse. Looking from the north side (cargo area) of the airport today, this hangar (the left of the two hangars on the south side) is still in use in its original form, being under the control of BAE SYSTEMS.

On 19 April 1953 a Glasgow (Renfrew)–Edinburgh–Birmingham–Northolt service was started by BEA using DC3s and Vickers Vikings. Later that year, at the Turnhouse Battle of Britain Open Day, the main attraction was the breaking of the sound barrier – which created a 'double boom' – during a display by a Royal Canadian Air Force Sabre F86A. This was the first time the sound barrier had been broken at an air display in Scotland.

In addition to 603 Squadron, 666 Air Observation Post Squadron (RAuxAF), equipped with Taylorcraft Austers, and the Station Communication Flight, comprising an Avro Anson and several Airspeed Oxfords, were stationed at Turnhouse in the mid-1950s.

Later in the 1950s, there were a growing number of UK airlines and aircraft types that could be seen at Turnhouse, including Tradair (Viscounts); Derby Airways, one of the forerunners of British Midland Airways (Handley Page Marathons); Continental Air Services (Vickers Vikings); Skyways (DC3s) and operating charters Curtis C–46 Commandos of Fred Olsen Lines. Tradair was incorporated into Channel Airways in December 1962 and Channel itself ceased trading in 1972.

DH Comet XK716 RAF Transport Command, 3 April 1958. (Gordon Pearson)

OE–FDA, Douglas DC3 Austrian Airlines, 4 September 1958. Eight months after this picture was taken at Turnhouse, OE-FDA hit the 3,300ft Alfabia Peak, Majorca on its return flight to Vienna from Palma, killing the two crew and three passengers on 2 May 1959. (Gordon Pearson)

Douglas DC3 belonging to the Israeli Airline ARKIA, c.1950s. (Gordon Pearson)

A Northolt–Birmingham–Edinburgh–Glasgow service was operated by BEA with Pionairs in the early 1950s, with flight BE 920 departing Northolt at 08.45 and the return flight (BE 925) departing at 18.20. However, Northolt ceased to be the London terminus for flights on 31 October 1954, and flights were transferred to Heathrow; the last arrival at Northolt from Turnhouse (via Glasgow and Birmingham) was flight BE 925, landing at 12.05 on 30 October 1954. A thrice-weekly service to Lerwick and a daily Aberdeen–Turnhouse–Heathrow service was operated by BEA from 1954–1957 (Pionairs were used until 1955, when they were replaced by Viscounts).

Up until this point passenger facilities at Turnhouse had been situated in an old RAF barrack block. On 27 July 1953, Air Commodore J.G. Murray, the Scottish Divisional Controller of the Ministry of Civil Aviation, announced plans to build a completely new civil terminal and apron on the north side of the airfield about a quarter of a mile

Aer Lingus Fokker F.27 EI–AKF, 1958. (Colin Lourie)

BOAC Canadair C.4 Argonaut G–ALHR, 1958. Named Antiope, this aircraft later flew with Aden Airways as VR–AAR. (Gordon Pearson)

Blackburn Beverly XL149 of 228 OCU 84 Squadron, Thorney Island, 19 September 1958. The cockpit of XL149 is now preserved at Aeroventure, Doncaster, South Yorks. (Gordon Pearson)

beyond the main RAF entrance. The estimated cost was £59,000, comprising £47,500 for the new building, £2,500 for new roads, and £9,000 for a new apron in front of the terminal. Part of the reason for the proposals was that the RAF had requested that the buildings currently in public use be transferred back to military ownership. The plans for the terminal were made by Professor Robert H. Matthew ARIBA, ARIAS who had recently been appointed to the chair of architecture at Edinburgh University and who had also designed the Royal Festival Hall on the South Bank of the river Thames.

In August 1954 work started on the new terminal building. The principal contractor was Nathaniel Grieve of Washington Lane, Edinburgh and the interior furnishings were designed by Prof. Matthew Alexander Harvey (Edinburgh) Ltd of 44 Queen Street, Edinburgh. The materials used were steel framing, reinforced concrete and African mahogany weatherboarding with large plate glass windows in aluminium frames, which gave the building a quite distinctive look. Inside, French beech panelling and teak were also used. The concourse was 2,000sq.ft, and on the ground floor were customs facilities, offices, check-in counters, a baggage hall and a bookstall. Stairs led to a first-floor buffet and bar. There were also first-class viewing facilities from an open first-floor roof terrace which also had its own exterior concrete stairs. The building was designed with ease of expansion in mind and was the third civil airport terminal to be built after the war by the Ministry of Transport and Civil Aviation (the others were Renfrew and London). At the time of its completion, the terminal was believed to be the largest wooden-exterior building in the UK and, despite the initial estimate of £59,000, the total final cost was £84,000. Mr Harold Watkinson MP, the Minister of Transport and Civil Aviation, opened the new facilities on 12 April 1956.

Traffic had grown considerably in the first part of the 1950s, particularly on the London route (a pattern that was to continue). In 1951, 16,000 passengers were recorded, followed by 31,000 in 1952, 43,000 in 1953, and 55,000 in 1954. The inauguration of the Viscount service by BEA on the London route gave a further boost to the figures, with a total of 70,000 passengers using the airport that year. The introduction of Viscounts on the London route led BEA to introduce the first-class 'Chieftain' service (the Glasgow–London service was named 'Clansman'). This was intended to be luxury travel with food and service to match, but it enjoyed only limited success and the service was dropped on all routes on which it had been trialled. The last international service was Paris–London in 1958, and all domestic services were curtailed by March 1960.

RAF Turnhouse was the scene of yet another speed record, set on 8 August 1956 when Squadron Leader R.L. Topp took off in a Hawker Hunter F4 (WT739) of 43 Squadron and covered the 331.6 miles between Turnhouse and RAF Northolt in 27 minutes 52.8 seconds, travelling at an average speed of 717.504mph. This record stood until July 1987.

As previously stated, the 10 May 1957 saw the disbandment of all twenty Royal Air Force Auxiliary Squadrons, including 603 Squadron. The squadron heard the news on the 6 January, which allowed enough time for a final flypast over Edinburgh, with seven Vampires and one Meteor taking part. The Squadron Standard was laid up at St Giles, Edinburgh, on 17 November 1957.

Bristol 170 G–AIFV, c.1950s. G–AIFV had previously been leased to Air Malta. (Gordon Pearson)

LN–FOS, Curtis C–46 Commando of Fred Olsen Lines, on a cargo charter. (Colin Lourie)

HP Hastings taxiing to take off from runway 13 on a troop-carrying flight. (Colin Lourie)

BKS Douglas DC3 G–AMVC, 1958. This aircraft operated the first BKS service out of Turnhouse to Belfast. (Gordon Pearson)

BKS Airspeed Ambassador later used on the Belfast route, replacing the DC3. (Colin Lourie)

Gloster Javelin XA710, 20 September 1958. Most of the new Javelins for 151 Squadron were delivered direct to Turnhouse while runway work was carried out at RAF Leuchars. (Gordon Pearson)

A fine study of Bristol Brigand T4 WA561 of 228 OCU on a visit to RAF Turnhouse, 1954. (J. Bricknall, ATCO)

OO–EHE Benes-Mraz Sokol (a Czech design), 6 August 1960. Pictured before the customs block extension was added to the original 1950s terminal building. (Colin Lourie)

In the world of civil aviation, BEA started a weekend service to Jersey on 9 June 1957 which operated during the summer months and was to prove a success. BKS, meanwhile, was one of the first independent airlines to start services, initially operating DC3s (the first flight being undertaken by G–AMVC) to Belfast on to Newcastle twice a week from 1956 to December 1961. The Edinburgh to Belfast portion of the service was operated three times a week from 23 May 1958 with Airspeed Ambassadors, increasing to a daily service in the peak summer months. A direct service to Newcastle from Belfast was opened in 1958, leaving the Edinburgh segment to operate only to Belfast. BKS suspended the Edinburgh service in December 1961 but resumed services a couple of years later.

Another airline operating during this period was Silver City which started an Isle of Man service on 1 June 1958, flying DH Herons and Bristol 170 Freighters on a Friday and Sunday. The Heron 1B was replaced by the DC3 from the 1960 summer season onwards.

In 1961 Turnhouse was closed in order for strengthening work to be carried out on runway 13/31. The strengthening would allow BEA to use the Vickers Vanguard on the Heathrow–Turnhouse route. During the period of closure, all flights were transferred to East Fortune airfield (23 miles to the east of Edinburgh). East Fortune was the site from which Airship R34 had set out on its historic Atlantic trip in July 1919, when it made the first ever east-to-west crossing, taking 108 hours for the journey. The airfield shared many similarities with Turnhouse. It had, for example, also started life as an RFC airfield station in 1915, had a 6,000ft runway, and had been used by the RAF. It was, however, between 40 minutes and an hour away from the city by road, therefore much further than Turnhouse, which was only about 20 minutes away. Preparation work was carried out by the Ministry of Civil Aviation and BEA at a cost of £40,000. The building used as a temporary terminal was a former office at BEA's engineering base which was dismantled, taken by road from London and reassembled at East Fortune. During the short period (four months) it was used as Edinburgh Airport, it handled 2,640 civil aircraft movements along with 96,000 passengers. One unfortunate incident took place on 26 May 1961, when an RAF Percival Pembroke (WV737) which had just brought Air Vice Marshals R.B. Simpson and R.H. Wright from a NATO meeting in Paris, crashed shortly after take-off on its way to RAF Leuchars, coming down at Newhouse Farm near North Berwick. The Pembroke was destroyed in the accident but miraculously no one was hurt. The Pembroke was flown by Flt Lt Munn and was normally based at RAF Turnhouse. Engine failure was given as the official cause of the accident. Turnhouse also received a 'new' control tower at this time. It had formerly been the Visual Control Room at the recently closed Blackbushe airport and was re-erected on top of the original wartime control tower at Turnhouse.

Another addition was a new customs block built in 1961 at a cost of £49,000. It was an extension to the south-east section of the terminal and gave a much needed improvement to the processing of customs formalities. It was connected to the main terminal by a smaller link block.

US Navy C–117 with the RAF officers' mess in the background. (Colin Lourie)

USOA (US Overseas Airlines) DC4 N90436, September 1961. (Colin Lourie)

London passengers boarding from the temporary passenger terminal at East Fortune while runway work was carried out at Turnhouse. (Museum of Flight, East Fortune)

Vickers Viscount 779 OE–LAD of Austrian Airlines, 7 September 1958. OE–LAD operated the first international service for Austrian Airlines from Vienna to London Heathrow on 31 March 1958. (Gordon Pearson)

Vickers Viscount 802 of Aer Lingus. (Gordon Pearson)

Vickers Viscount 802 G–AOHI of BEA, Charles Montague Doughty, named after the explorer and author, 4 September 1958. (Gordon Pearson)

BEA started operating Vanguards (two daily) to back up the Viscounts on the Heathrow route after the runway work on 13/31 was completed at Turnhouse and flights were transferred back from East Fortune. A study in 1962 found that 10 per cent of 113 Vanguard flights were diverted due to crosswinds. This was double the rate of the ICAO standard which should be necessary for a properly equipped airport.

There were many 'firsts' after the re-opening of Turnhouse on completion of the main runway work. A new service to Exeter was started on 2 June 1962 with the first flight flown by a Viscount 714. This was G–ARIR, belonging to Tradair. The first visit of a jet transport was on 9 February 1963 when an Air France Caravelle (F–BHRR) arrived. G–APET was the first of many BEA Vanguards to use Turnhouse after the runway work was complete.

A name that was to become synonymous with flying in Scotland (Loganair) started life at Edinburgh on 1 February 1962 as the air taxi service of the Logan Construction Company with a single Piper Aztec (G–ASER). From this modest beginning, Loganair expanded its fleet and route network in addition to the air taxi role. The airline carved a niche for itself, particularly on services to the Highlands and Islands. In November 1963 Loganair, under a dispensation from the Ministry of Aviation, operated a charter service, in conjunction with Mackay Bros & Co. (Dundee) Ltd, from Dundee's Riverside airport, which connected with BEA's 07.50 departure to Heathrow and the 09.20 arrival from Heathrow. The fare was £1 10s single and £3 return if five passengers were carried. A single passenger could charter the Aztec for £15 return. This service was later regularised with the ATLB. Loganair also developed a relationship with the Scottish Ambulance Service which continues to this day, providing 24-hour ambulance services to the remote communities. The ambulance services started later, in 1967, serving Coll,

Colonsay, Oronsay, Mull and Oban. Despite having started at Turnhouse, Loganair gradually made Glasgow its main base of operations although flights continued to be operated from Edinburgh.

From the spring of 1962, BEA introduced three Handley Page Heralds on its Scottish routes, replacing the Pionairs. One service was routed from Glasgow (Renfrew) through Turnhouse to Aberdeen, Wick, Orkney, and return, in addition to a Glasgow (Renfrew) to Turnhouse and Aberdeen service. The Heralds were replaced in turn by Viscounts when BEA made their Scottish operation 'all Viscount' in the 1966–67 period. As for the London route, Vanguards had completely replaced Viscounts by summer 1962, producing a 21 per cent increase in growth.

A near-fatal accident was narrowly avoided on 11 April 1962 when Vanguard G–APEF, flown by Captain Dennis Clifton on flight No.BE5427 to Heathrow, hit a large flock of seagulls after take-off from Turnhouse shortly before midnight, causing two engines to fail immediately. The aircraft returned and had just made an emergency landing when the third engine failed. There was substantial damage to the aircraft but fortunately no casualties among the sixty-nine passengers and crew. The wind and rain on that night did not make things any easier for Captain Clifton.

BUA (British United Airways) were granted a licence in 1962 to operate a service to Gatwick. Also in 1962, BKS were granted a licence to operate services between Edinburgh and Leeds, but never chose to fly the route.

On 17 October 1962 a DH Heron of the Queen's Flight, carrying Premier Harold Macmillan and five passengers, was involved in an emergency. Just after take-off from Turnhouse for RAF Benson, the pilot, Squadron Leader D.M. Diver, was informed by the control tower that his undercarriage had not fully raised. He managed to land safely and, after the fault was repaired, they resumed their journey. No fewer than eight ambulances

Bristol Sycamore HR14 XJ917. (Gordon Pearson)

Two Vickers Varsities parked at the RAF apron. The ex-Blackbushe control tower is clearly visible in the background. (Colin Lourie)

Hiller 360 G–AOFV, equipped for crop-spraying (registration crudely painted on the chemical tank), operated by Helicopter Services, 27 August 1962. (Colin Lourie)

Royal Navy Westland S51 Dragonfly WG724 in front of the control tower, 8 June 1962. Note the tail of the Javelin in the background. This Dragonfly was Lossiemouth-based. (Colin Lourie)

Douglas DC4 F–BORJ of the French operator TAI, caught in the early morning sunlight, operating a rugby charter, 13 January 1962. (Colin Lourie)

responded to the emergency call, along with three fire engines. A note in the evening paper mentioned that there were still more than twelve two-man ambulances available for emergency calls in Edinburgh despite eight vehicles being sent at the airport. Mr Macmillan had been in Edinburgh making arrangements for King Olav's visit.

In 1963, Turnhouse had some unusual equipment added to the ends of the main runway (13/31), in the form of arrester barriers. Costing £2,000, they were 200ft wide, made of elastic and fitted to the overshoot areas. They were intended for high-speed military aircraft such as the Buccaneer, which could be stopped by the barriers within 450ft when travelling at 90mph. They were kept in a 'flat' position but could be raised instantly if the need arose. They were not suitable for propeller aircraft.

A standby fare was introduced by BEA in 1963 on all its trunk routes from Heathrow to Glasgow and Turnhouse. There was a discount of one-third on the normal fare, the only stipulation being that a passenger could not pre-book and had to turn up at the airport to be carried only if there was a spare seat available. This proved to be so popular the standby fare concept was extended to a number of other domestic routes.

The 1960s were also a period of sustained growth for Turnhouse. Passenger numbers had grown to over 454,000 in 1964, a great increase on ten years earlier, when the total was only 55,000.

Although the Highlands and Islands destinations have always had a comprehensive coverage from Glasgow (using BEA Herons designated for the Highlands and Islands services G–ANXA and G–ANXB), there had also been services to a number of these destinations from Edinburgh. In 1962 a daily service (Monday to Friday) was operated on the route Renfrew–Turnhouse–Inverness–Wick–Kirkwall. A later service to Inverness operated by BEA from 1 April 1967 was stopped on 9 June 1969 due to poor loads.

HP Herald, one of three used on the Scottish routes. (Colin Lourie)

RAF Bristol Britannia about to turn on to runway 13. (Colin Lourie)

Aer Lingus eventually replaced the DC3 on the Dublin route with the F.27 Fokker Friendship in January 1964. The F.27s were later replaced by the larger Viscounts in the 1960s as passenger numbers started to grow.

On 11 May 1964 BKS flew the Ambassador on the Edinburgh–Belfast run, restarting the service. The standard fare charged in 1966 was £4 17s. On 31 October 1968 BKS operated its last Belfast to Edinburgh flight before the service was handed over to Cambrian Airways as a swap with the Liverpool–Belfast route. At this time BKS also became responsible for handling all Cambrian Airways aircraft at Heathrow. British Eagle was another well-known airline from this period. On 9 April 1962 both British Eagle and BUA applied for licences on a number of UK routes, to operate from Heathrow (British Eagle) and Gatwick (BUA). BEA strongly opposed the applications granted to British Eagle and BUA. After an appeal by BEA lasting eleven days, they were only successful in stopping two of the licence applications. British Eagle were granted permission to operate a daily Heathrow service from Turnhouse and this started on 4 November 1963 using Bristol Britannias, with G–AOVT operating the first flight. Initially a daily service was the maximum frequency permitted but later this increased to ten flights a week. A sales office and town terminal was opened at 27 George Street, Edinburgh. British Eagle also looked at the possibility of an Edinburgh–Manchester or Edinburgh–Birmingham service in 1965 but this did not materialise. There were heavy development costs on the London–Scotland trunk routes of between £300,000 and £350,000 and the now twice-daily Britannia service was reduced to one daily Viscount service in 1965. Unfortunately, this was still not economically viable without higher frequencies and, sadly, the service was withdrawn on 20 February 1965. The airline itself folded on 6 November 1968.

Bristol Britannia of Cunard Eagle, used on the relatively short-lived Heathrow route. Two Starways Douglas DC6s in background. (Colin Lourie)

USAF C–97 0–59595. (Colin Lourie)

Two Air France Caravelles operating rugby charter flights. (Colin Lourie)

PA22 Caribbean G–APXS in 1960, when US light civil aircraft were beginning to make their presence felt in the UK. (Colin Lourie)

Cambrian Airways were regular visitors throughout the 1960s flying rugby charters and training flights with Viscounts as well as operating a Belfast (Aldergrove)–Turnhouse service in the late 1960s and early 1970s.

From the mid-1960s right up until the BAA takeover in 1971 there was a period of great dissatisfaction and controversy over the facilities at Turnhouse. In the early 1960s, there was a realisation that crosswinds were a problem at Turnhouse and, as early as September 1963, proposals had been made for a new runway. A chart released at the time showed the position and alignment of a 7,000ft runway in exactly the position the new runway was to occupy thirteen years later. Turnhouse was described in 1965 as the fastest growing airport in the UK. However, crosswinds in one week in March 1967 caused the diversion and cancellation of fifty-nine scheduled flights (equivalent to 27 per cent of all scheduled flights that week).

Some comments from that period will illustrate the views on both sides of the debate regarding new facilities and a new runway: on 8 March 1965 Roy Jenkins, the Minister of Aviation, announced in the House of Commons that he was not convinced spending £2–3 million on a new runway would be justified. Then, on 23 March 1966, Jim Telfer (Liberal candidate for Edinburgh West), at a meeting at Royston School, said the refusal to build a second runway at Turnhouse was 'a typical piece of Tory and Socialist neglect of Scotland's interests'. Sir John Toothill, chairman and general manager of Ferranti, and author of the Toothill report on Scotland's economy, was reported as saying on 29 November 1966 that, 'Edinburgh could have the worst airport in Europe'. In a written Commons reply to Anthony Stodart MP (Conservative, Edinburgh West) on 21 July 1966, Roy Mason, the Minister of State at the Board of Trade, denied that facilities at the airport were inadequate. In 1965, Corporation Treasurer H.A. Brechin adopted the same view as his predecessor, Treasurer Will Darling, had in the late 1930s, stating that he was not prepared to saddle the Edinburgh ratepayers with the expense, maintaining that the cost should be borne by the government. After a visit to both Turnhouse and Prestwick in September 1965, Roy Jenkins stated that the ministry was prepared to consider a new

Avro 19 Anson of BKS Air Survey. Many Ansons found their way into civilian use after the war. This particular aircraft is under restoration at the Museum of Flight, East Fortune. (Colin Lourie) Internet details: http://www.apss.org.uk/projects/anson/index.htm)

Hunting Percival Pembroke WV737 in RAF hangar at Turnhouse. This was the aircraft which crashed and burned out shortly after taking off from East Fortune on 26 May 1961. (Colin Lourie)

Hunting Percival Pembroke WV739 landing on the shorter 08/26 runway. Based at Turnhouse but also based at RAF Ballykelly (Station Flight) in the 1960s. (Colin Lourie)

US Navy WV–2. These aircraft were fairly regular visitors into Turnhouse. (Colin Lourie)

Bristol 170 G–AGPV Trans European Airways. This was the prototype Bristol Freighter and first flew on 2 December 1945. It was then used in service trials at Boscombe Down, as a result of which the wingspan was increased by 3.05m, allowing a higher gross weight, which needed more powerful engines. (Colin Lourie)

£750,000 terminal, but would not look at building a new runway for at least ten years. Wing Commander Dalgleish added his voice to the debate in March 1966 by saying that East Fortune would be better developed as the airport for Edinburgh instead of Turnhouse. A newspaper report in February 1967 criticised the lack of surveillance radar at Turnhouse; J.P. Mallalieu (Minister of State at the BOT) said in February 1967 that delays at Turnhouse were due to crosswinds rather than the lack of radar. Finally, on top of all this, a long-running dispute between Edinburgh Corporation and the Board of Trade continued, with the Board demanding that Edinburgh Corporation should take over Turnhouse, and the Edinburgh Corporation refusing to do this unless the Board first paid for and provided the new facilities required at the airport. The stalemate continued right up until the entry of the BAA on the scene.

Unusual airlines operating into Turnhouse on an irregular basis during the 1960s included Tyne Tees Aviation (DC3), Hunting Air Surveys (DC3), Starways (Viscount 700), Eros Airlines (Viscount 700), CSA Czechoslovakian Airlines (IL18 & Britannia), Scanair (DC7), Transair Sweden (DC7), Flying Enterprise Denmark (DC6 & DC7), British Westpoint (DC3), Osterman Air Sweden (DC7), Gregory Air Service (DC3), JAT (CV440), Rhodesian Air Service (DC4), Braathens SAFE (F.27 & DC6). Alitalia operated the DC9, and the airline flew the Italian President to Scotland on 9 April 1969. Besides regular visits from RAF aircraft (including Britannias for trooping flights), there were regular visits by aircraft from all the NATO air arms. Unusual military visitors included a visit from two Zambian Air Force DH5s in June 1965.

In an attempt to improve its service for business passengers, BEA introduced a coach service in 1965 to run from its West London Air Terminal in Kensington to the steps of the aircraft and vice versa. It was primarily aimed at businessmen with hand baggage only on BEA's main trunk routes from Heathrow to Turnhouse, Glasgow, Belfast and Aberdeen. Called the 'Executive Express' it proved to be very popular, carrying 1,000 passengers in its first week.

A crowded apron scene in June 1966. (Colin Lourie)

Apron scene. USAF Douglas C-124 Globemaster II with the Pentland Hills forming the backdrop.

The Beatles arriving on 19 October 1964. They played at the ABC in Lothian Road and were riding on the success of *A Hard Day's Night.* The single had topped the charts a couple of months previously, and the LP was still at the top of the charts. (Scotsman Archives)

Marlene Dietrich and Burt Bacharach arriving at Turnhouse on 22 August 1965. Although a respected composer in his own right, Burt Bacharach was an arranger, pianist and band leader for Marlene Dietrich. (Scotsman Archives)

BUA (British United Airways) started what later proved to be a very popular Gatwick service. The first flight was flown by BAC 1–11 G–ASJJ on 4 January 1966 (G–ASJI having completed a proving flight just prior to this on 13 December 1965). The service grew to five daily flights on weekdays and three on Saturdays and Sundays. BUA operated a daily limousine service to and from Dundee to connect with these flights for a brief experimental period. Two other routes operated by BUIA (BUIA, a subsidiary of BUA, was formed from the merger of Jersey Airlines and Silver City Airways in 1962, later merging with Morton Air Services in 1968 and renaming itself British Island Airways in 1970) were to the Isle of Man in the summer months (June–September) using DC3s, and to Southampton via Abbotsinch using Viscounts (once weekly). The Edinburgh–Isle of Man route was operated every summer by BUIA (after the merger with Silver City, who had previously operated the route). After a period of financial difficulty BUA was bought by Caledonian Airways on 30 September 1970, temporarily merging as 'Caledonian/BUA' before the title British Caledonian was settled upon. British Caledonian itself was later absorbed into British Airways.

From September 1966, Strathallan Air Services Ltd (trading as Strathair) operated a twice-daily Dundee–Edinburgh–Prestwick–Edinburgh–Dundee service using a DC3 and a

DH Dove (G–ASDD). The DC3 (G–APPO) was based at Turnhouse from 15 May 1966. The airline had started operations in December 1964 with a single Helio Courier which was replaced in turn by the Dove and a Piper Aztec (G–ATLC, owned by Scottish Malt Distillers Ltd) and Piper Twin Comanche (G–ATWG, owned by West Highland Woodlands Ltd), plus the DC3. The Dundee–Edinburgh–Prestwick service was operated for only six weeks before it was withdrawn due to a lack of support. In 1967, Strathair had a licence to operate an Inverness–Dundee–Edinburgh service. In August of that year, they applied to the ATLB (Air Transport Licensing Board) to vary the licence so that Dundee was not a compulsory stop. They held two licences and had already withdrawn from the Edinburgh–Dundee route. The request was granted, to take effect from 1 September 1967 despite opposition from BEA who said it would divert passengers from their Edinburgh–Inverness service.

Brantly B2B G–ASXE. (Robert Whitton)

Avro 19 Anson G–AGWE being refuelled. This Anson continued its 'career' in museums in Scotland, England and the USA. (Robert Whitton)

Cessna 150 G–APZR. (Robert Whitton)

DH Comet in Olympic Airways colours. (Colin Lourie)

HS 748 of Luton-based carrier Autair. (Colin Lourie)

A fine head-on picture of a Cambrian Airways Viscount which was operating a Welsh rugby charter. (Colin Lourie)

US Navy C–131F parked by the RAF hangars. (Colin Lourie)

US Navy Grumman C–1A Trader of VRC–40 Squadron. (Colin Lourie)

Rugby charter flights for international matches were a feature of Edinburgh (and still are). An example is 2–6 February 1967, when twenty-one Viscount charter flights and fourteen DC3 charter flights were flown to carry people to and from a match against Wales.

The year 1967 also saw another emergency involving a VIP, when an Andover of the Queen's Flight carrying the Duke of Edinburgh landed at Turnhouse with its starboard engine out of action. The aircraft was on its way to Aberdeen when it developed engine problems over Lockerbie. The aircraft was repaired at RAF Turnhouse and the Duke continued his journey to Balmoral by car.

A detailed study of Turnhouse was carried out in 1967 by four pupils from Fettes College in Edinburgh. Their statistical breakdown of passengers showed the changing face of air travel and stated quite correctly that the lowering of air fares and introduction of larger and more economical aircraft would 'lead to enormous potential for internal air travel'. They also found that less than half of the passengers interviewed actually came from Edinburgh itself and went on to say that a Central Scotland Airport would have been more beneficial. One woman interviewed said she preferred flying in Vanguards and Viscounts to jets as 'there was more chance of survival at 350mph than 600mph'. Ironically, despite all the controversy over the adequacy of airport facilities at this time, the survey found that 80 per cent of passengers interviewed were entirely happy with the airport.

BEA used DH Comets on the route to Heathrow for a temporary period in the late 1960s, starting on 16 January 1967, and also operated a daily service to Manchester and Birmingham with Viscounts. There were two daily Heathrow flights by the Comets at peak times, one in the morning and an evening flight which cut the travelling time by 15 minutes. One Viscount operator at this time was British Midland Airways (BMA), operating flights to Castle Donington (now East Midlands Airport). The British Midland service to Castle Donington started on 3 October 1967 with eight weekly flights and proved a success.

The first recorded visit by a Trident to Turnhouse was on 4 August 1968 when Trident II G–AVFF flew a Heathrow service in place of a Vanguard. The event had been mentioned in the *Edinburgh Evening News* a few days prior to the aircraft's arrival, and a large crowd had gathered in the viewing area. Another first visit in the same month was a Lufthansa Boeing 737 (D–ABEF) which arrived on 30 August from Hamburg and departed to Frankfurt. Another Lufthansa Boeing 737 (D–ABEO) visited a week later, on 6 September.

A new and short-lived service was operated by Air Ulster in 1968, flying from Edinburgh to Londonderry (Northern Ireland) via Glasgow. The service was initially operated by a DC3, and later by a Viscount leased from Aer Lingus (EI–APD). The airport used for Londonderry was RAF Ballykelly instead of Eglinton. Air Ulster ceased operations in 1970.

In a throwback to the earlier days of flying, the summer weekends of 1969 saw the public enjoying pleasure flights from Turnhouse over the Forth Bridges and Edinburgh Castle for 25s in a Cessna 172 Skyhawk.

Dutch Navy Lockheed P2V–7 Neptune. (Colin Lourie)

DC3 PH–SCC of Dutch airline Martins Air Charter. (Colin Lourie)

TF–ISC Douglas DC6B of Icelandair, July 1966. (Colin Lourie)

West German Navy Percival Sea Prince 2, August 1966. (Colin Lourie)

An excellent night-time shot of BUA BAC 1–11 G–ASJF in January 1967, when the introduction of BEA Comets brought direct jet competition on the London–Edinburgh route. (Colin Lourie)

An innovative idea for its time was the introduction by Channel Airways of its Scottish Flyer Service in 1969, using Viscounts and the HS.748. Although the service was mainly operated with Viscounts, the proving flight on 9 October 1967 was actually operated by BAC 1–11 G–AVGP. The service itself did not start until 20 January 1969, when Viscount 800 G–AVHK flew the first flight. It was billed as 'Britain's first city to city through air service'. Originating at the Channel Airways base in Southend, the service continued to Luton, Castle Donington (East Midlands), Leeds/Bradford, Teesside, Newcastle, Edinburgh, Aberdeen and return. After less than a year, the service was unfortunately suspended on 28 November 1971, after Channel Airways had incurred losses of £160,000 on the route.

Iberia operated Caravelles in the summer of 1969, starting on 7 June to run to 30 September. There was a flight every Saturday as a preliminary attempt to test the holiday market to Spain. The flight was to Barcelona and Palma and cost £45 return. As it was the airport's first scheduled direct link to the continent, things did not go smoothly. The flight on 16 August 1969 was diverted to Glasgow because of a risk that emergency services would not be available for its take-off on the return flight. The problem was that Turnhouse officially closed at 9.50 p.m., and Iberia were paying a 150 per cent surcharge on handling fees for the airport to remain open until its ETA of 10.40 p.m. and ETD

Morane Saulnier Paris, French Navy, parked at the RAF apron, 29 March 1967. (Colin Lourie)

Busy apron scene, August 1967. (Gordon Pearson)

BEA DH Comet G–APME. (Robert Whitton)

An atmospheric picture of passengers boarding a Heathrow-bound Comet. (Robert Whitton)

The tail of a US-registered Grumman Gulfstream executive jet with a BEA Comet and Cambrian Airways Viscount. (Robert Whitton)

US Douglas DC6 and Grumman Gulfstream I. (Robert Whitton)

A West German Air Force Convair CV 440, serial 12 + 02, c.1968. This particular CV 440 had a long career, also flying for owners in the USA, Norway and Mexico, as well as the WG Air Force. (Robert Whitton)

A BEA Vanguard on a wet Edinburgh day. (BA Museum & Archives)

of 11.30 p.m. However, it transpired that Iberia had not been told there was a strict 15-minute leeway time (imposed by the Board of Trade who controlled the airport) for the return flight at 11.30 p.m. If this leeway time was exceeded then the emergency services watch would not be extended, and the aircraft would be stranded until Sunday morning. Iberia's flight on the 16 August had diverted rather than take the risk. Although the earlier flights had been trouble-free, Iberia decided to cancel the remaining four flights of the season. Stanley Ballantine, the manager of Iberia Scotland stated that the 15-minute margin was not enough, due to the inadequacy of services at Turnhouse. There was not a large enough bowser to bring all the fuel required in one trip; sometimes it took a long time to close the public road when runway 13 was used for take-off, and incoming passengers had to go through customs first before outgoing passengers could be processed. Mr Ballantine also said that firemen wanted a bonus payment for the later hours. This was denied by James Halley, the airport commandant, who blamed Iberia for any delays. This in turn was denied by Mr Ballantine. Iberia did not repeat the experiment. A series of wildcat strikes by porters and firemen at the end of 1968 and the beginning of 1969 did little to help the airport's reputation.

BEA Vanguard taking off for Heathrow from runway 13. (BA Museum & Archives)

'Rent-a-Copter' Hughes 269B G–ASTZ. (Robert Whitton)

US-registered F.27. (Robert Whitton)

8 August 1968. Swiss Lear Jet HB–VBA – Jim Clark, the former World Racing Champion was tragically killed in a 170mph crash in a Formula Two race the previous day at Hockenheim. Jimmy Lyon (with hat) was Jim Clark's lawyer. Just behind him is Alex Calder, who used to race, and who was married to Jim Clark's oldest sister, Mattie. They were flying to Germany to sort out the legal arrangements for the return of Jim's body. HB–VBA made two trips into Edinburgh that day. (Colin Lourie)

Aer Lingus switched from Viscounts in the late 1960s and early 1970s on the Dublin route to using Boeing 737s and BAC 1–11s. Air Anglia started its first scheduled service on 7 December 1970 with a BN Islander from its base at Norwich to Aberdeen via Turnhouse. Air Anglia's aircraft were a regular feature at the airport and a twice-daily Edinburgh–Amsterdam service was started in 1975. They later merged with Air Wales, BIA and Westward to form Air UK.

7
BEA Vanguard Crash 1965

Despite the commendable reliability and good safety record of the Vickers Vanguard (it had, up until 1965, carried 26 million passengers without any fatalities), 1965 saw the first major crash involving the aircraft. On the night of 27 October 1965, BEA Vanguard (G–APEE) was on the last scheduled flight of the day from Turnhouse to Heathrow. Captain Norman Shackell and his crew had operated the previous night flight from Palma to Heathrow, arriving at Heathrow at 5.30 a.m. After 13 hours off-duty they returned as stand-by crew to take the 8.00 p.m. flight to Edinburgh when the rostered crew were delayed by weather. On the return leg to Heathrow they took off from Turnhouse at 11.17 p.m. and arrived over London on schedule, but were asked to hold in a stack because of bad weather. Although there was fog, it was felt that conditions were acceptable for landing. After holding in the stack for 55 minutes, Captain Shackell attempted to land twice but overshot on both occasions. He then made his third and final attempt. As the Vanguard touched the runway, it slewed off and crashed, bursting into flames. Sadly, everyone on board was killed (thirty passengers and six crew). Councillor John F. Stewart, proprietor of Stewart's Ballroom at Abbeyhill, was among the dead, as was a Newhaven woman making her first flight with her daughter and eighteen-month-old grandson. Also killed were John Ross of Craigcrook Road, who worked for the Scottish Grocers' Federation, and Ann Plummer of Great Junction Street, Leith. Both of these passengers had considered themselves 'lucky' to get standby seats on the flight. Condolences were sent by the Queen and Sir James Miller, the Lord Mayor of London (and a former Lord Provost of Edinburgh). An inquiry into the crash discounted the theory that debris had been on the runway, and the cause was stated as pilot error. G–APEE was an unfortunate aircraft; on 6 October in the year before its fatal accident, it had suffered a collapsed nose-wheel after a heavy landing at Glasgow.

The ill-fated Vanguard G–APEE seen in happier circumstances, parked in front of the Queen's Building at Heathrow. (BA Museum & Archives)

Another view of Vanguard G–APEE, this time at a wet Turnhouse. (Colin Lourie)

8
BAA Takeover

In its fourth year, the BAA (British Airports Authority) began talks with the Board of Trade to take over and manage Turnhouse. The BAA owned four airports (Heathrow, Gatwick, Stansted and Prestwick) at this time, and saw Turnhouse as a useful addition to its portfolio and an opportunity to expand its operations in Scotland beyond Prestwick, which it already owned.

In 1969 Turnhouse was the ninth busiest UK airport, handling over 600,000 passengers, and was the fourth busiest UK airport (after Heathrow, Gatwick and Glasgow) in terms of aircraft movements (55,983). The years 1969 and 1970 passed without any decision by the Government about the proposed transfer but, on the 28 May 1970, in reply to a question in the House of Commons, the president of the Board of Trade said:

> The need for a major new terminal complex at Turnhouse Airport to cater for traffic growth has already been accepted. The siting of the new terminal has, however, been dependant on the nature of runway development to be undertaken.
>
> In view of the importance of Turnhouse Airport to the continuation of good air communications to Edinburgh and East Central Scotland, the government have decided that a new main runway should be provided at Turnhouse together with the new terminal complex. The new runway should almost entirely eliminate diversions from the airport on account of crosswind.
>
> A provisional agreement was reached two years ago between the Board of Trade and the British Airports Authority about the terms of a transfer of responsibility for Turnhouse Airport to the authority. Discussions with the BAA will now be resumed as a matter of urgency as it is the government's intention that, subject to planning permission and land purchase, the above developments should be completed as soon as practicable.

The British Airports Authority took over Turnhouse on 1 April 1971. Passenger numbers by this time were 666,329 (in the 1970/71 financial year) and the terminal was struggling to cope with the increased numbers. BAA immediately set about making a number of small changes (mainly cosmetic) shortly after their takeover. For instance nose-in parking for the aircraft was introduced, the buffet area had an internal wall removed, and the layout was changed in an attempt to improve seating capacity. TV monitors were also

Interior of original terminal building. (BA Museum & Archives)

Interior of original terminal building. Check-in desks on the left, main entrance on the
right and newsagents at the end of the picture. (BA Museum & Archives)

introduced in order to give flight information. This information had previously been
displayed on a board by the check-in desks which used plastic letters and numerals and
was altered by hand! Despite the small changes introduced at this time, the terminal was
deemed inadequate to meet future projected growth.

The main runway (13/31) with an inadequate length suffered constant diversions and
cancellations due to crosswinds. In addition the B9080 road had to be closed for landings
and take-offs on runway 13. Landing and take-offs on the 6,000ft 13/31 runway were a
tricky affair, as Peter Whittle, a former BEA Trident pilot explains:

I was a Trident pilot with the then BEA. I went to Edinburgh many times and it was always exciting. The runway (before the new runway and terminal was built in, I think, the late 70s) was very short for a Trident which was not the most powerful aircraft in either brakes or engines. In fact the Trident 3 used to have a boost engine fitted in the tail which was only used for short runways until about 500 agl and which many people thought was only put in for Edinburgh take offs! Landing was even more exciting as the only way to stop before the end of the runway was to engage reverse thrust before touch down. It was actually a very tricky manoeuvre because you need to do a much more vigorous flare than normal otherwise the firm touchdown needed (so you could apply the brakes quickly) would become a real thump. As you can imagine, this was quite scary for passengers not used to it. I remember one Edinburgh night-stop when we were in the bar and I overheard some Americans who had come in on the same flight talking about it in horror. Because of the difficulty it was nearly always a Captain's landing. I used to think it was marginal safety-wise. Several examples occurred of over-runs, most of them management pilots who were not well enough practiced. Of course as soon as the new runway and terminal was built all the fun went out of the trip and it just became another boring night stop.

Plans were proposed for a completely new runway and terminal building. A number of options for the new runway were examined, including an extension to 13/31 (the maximum length possible given the constraints was 7400ft) along with the possibility of a slight realignment. In the end a completely new runway 8400ft long on an alignment of 07/25 was deemed the most suitable option, along with associated taxiways to link up with the new terminal building and associated apron areas. The area chosen for the runway was land to the west of the airport. The terminal was to be built to the east of the new runway and south-west of the current airport boundary. The development would effectively double the size of the airport area.

There were many objections to the new proposals, primarily from residents living in Barnton and Cramond who were to live under the flightpath on the approach to the proposed runway 25. A public enquiry lasting nearly four months was held, starting on

Not a Trident and not Edinburgh, but this Air Koryo IL62 well illustrates the principle of reverse thrust being applied before touch down, as described by Peter Whittle. (Raymond Wang)

Laker Airways DC 10. (Colin Lourie)

1 November 1971 and finishing on 3 February 1972. This was one of the longest planning enquiries ever held in Scotland, and a period of thirteen months was to elapse before the publication of its findings in March 1973. One of the items put forward by the principal objectors (the Cramond Association) was that both Glasgow (Abbotsinch) and Edinburgh airports along with Prestwick be closed, to be replaced by a Central Scotland Airport (CSA) to be built midway between Glasgow and Edinburgh with an 11,000ft runway to serve the Central Scotland region as well as Glasgow and Edinburgh. Airth was suggested as a possible location. This option was eventually rejected but the reporter at the enquiry felt the case had merit and deserved further examination. The subject of a Central Scotland Airport was raised again prior to the announcement of the aviation white paper in December 2003. Surprisingly, the reporter who conducted the inquiry (Mr G.S. Gimson QC) rejected the application for the expansion, giving three reasons: a) the inclusion in the public safety zone at Newbridge of an existing population of about 500 persons, plus road users; b) the effect of aircraft noise at Newbridge; c) the effect of aircraft noise at Cramond. The Secretary of State for Scotland over-ruled the decision and gave his approval for the long-awaited expansion to start. An appeal by the main objectors was also over-ruled by Mr Gordon Campbell. On 19 January 1974 in a House of Commons statement, Mr Campbell stated that he had studied the report on Turnhouse by the Parliamentary Commission, and that the PCA found no grounds for criticising the way in which this very difficult planning issue had been handled by his officials in the Scottish Development Department. This confirmed for the Secretary of State the view that there were no grounds for reconsidering the planning permission granted for the developments. He also rejected a proposal put forward by the PCA to make an exceptional consideration for meeting the expenses of the main objector.

CL44 delivering newspapers during a strike in November 1979. (Colin Lourie)

F–BVFC. The first visit of a Concorde to Edinburgh, March 1980. (Robert Pittuck)

G–BOAE. The last visit of a Concorde to Edinburgh, 24 October 2003. (Allen McLaughlin)

Terminal building landside. (James O'Sullivan)

Another landside view of the terminal. (James O'Sullivan)

The South Apron. The new pier is being built to provide easier access and more passenger amenities for this apron. (James O'Sullivan)

CSA Boeing 737- 55S OK-DGL in an eye-catching livery to celebrate the airline's eightieth anniversary. (Allen McLaughlin)

Air Scotland Boeing 757-200, operated by Greece Airways with the Greek registration SX-BLW. (Allen McLaughlin)

Arrival of the Red Arrows from a display at East Fortune. (Colin Lourie)

South Cargo Apron. (Colin Lourie)

UM Air A320- 211 UR–UFB bringing football supporters of Shaktar Donetsk of Ukraine for a match against Celtic in Glasgow. (Glenn Surtees)

BEA formed a Scottish Airways Division in 1971 with two DH Herons (previously mentioned) and eight Viscounts. All these aircraft had the word 'Scottish' alongside the BEA logo on the fuselage. They operated all Scottish internal routes along with Glasgow–Belfast and Aberdeen and Inverness to Heathrow.

The BOAC/British Airways feeder service to Prestwick for North Atlantic flights was extended to Aberdeen from Edinburgh in December 1972. It operated until March 1976 with Viscounts G–AMOG (Golly) and G–AMON (Molly) and flew Belfast–Prestwick as well. They were later renamed 'Scottish Prince' and 'Scottish Princess' respectively. Both were chartered from Cambrian Airways and were ex-BEA aircraft. The service was later taken over by British Midland Airways.

The early 1970s saw BEA phasing out first-class travel on its domestic services, and this was finally completed on 1 February 1972. A limited number of first-class seats had been available on certain Trident and Vanguard services to Edinburgh (and Glasgow/Belfast) but demand tailed off and the service was stopped on 31 March 1972. For those wanting extra legroom and comfort, bookable seats were available, for a £2 supplement, in the rear compartment of the Vanguards and in the forward cabins of the Tridents. If the passengers were flying onwards from Heathrow by first class, these seats were free. BEA and BOAC were finally merged into British Airways on 31 March 1974. BEA and BOAC were dissolved and from that date British Airways flights into Edinburgh replaced BEA.

Work started on the initial stages of redevelopment of the airport in June 1973 including the diversion of the river Almond. The B9080, Eastfield Road and Hallyards Road were subject to a highways order closing them off to allow the development to take place. While the decision on redevelopment was awaited during 1972/73, congestion got worse, especially at peak periods, to the extent that the terminal was handling no less than eight times its design capacity. Further modifications were made to try and improve conditions, despite the confined space available. Two offices were removed in the arrivals hall to provide more space and the customs area was rearranged for better flow paths and to speed up the handling of international flights. Additionally, a new baggage system was installed in the arrivals hall using motorized baggage belts. The bar area was considerably extended and the restaurant and buffet were also improved with new furniture placed in each to give new higher density seating. Outside the terminal, extensive rearrangements were made to the approach roads and forecourt to improve passenger set-down and pick-up facilities. Space for this remodelling was found at the cost of forty spaces in the main car park. An overflow car park to the north of the B9080 road was then constructed to provide an additional 150 spaces. The bus stance was also re-positioned. One casualty of the new development was the Aeroville Lodge, which had seen use as the quarters of the commanding officer at RAF Turnhouse.

BAA Leaflet c.1972/73.
(BAA/W. Dunbar)

Flying into and out of Edinburgh Airport

Edinburgh Airport is served all the year round by British European Airways, with flights that link the capital with London (Heathrow), the major English cities of Manchester and Birmingham and with Glasgow, Aberdeen, Wick and Orkney. In summer, a service also makes direct flights to Jersey, one of the Channel Islands.

Caledonian-BUA operate daily jet services to London (Gatwick).

Cambrian Airways link Edinburgh with Belfast and a jet feeder service by Aer Lingus, allows trans-Atlantic travellers to fly on from Dublin.

A BOAC feeder flight provides a similar service from June to September for North American travellers who use Prestwick Airport.

And Air Anglia, operating with Islander aircraft, link the Scottish capital with the cathedral town of Norwich.

Left and opposite: BAA Leaflet c.1972/73. (BAA/W. Dunbar)

Facilities

Edinburgh Airport at present has a small, compact terminal, which means that passengers gain quick access to the aircraft and avoid the long, familiar walk to a distant aircraft stand.

For the arriving passenger, baggage reclaim and car hire desks stand side by side at the east end of the building. Check-in desks for all flights are a few yards from the doors where cars, taxis and coaches set down their passengers. And attractive buffet, restaurant, bar and bookstall facilities are knit together at the west end of the terminal, next to the observation terrace.

PARKING. National Car Parks Ltd., operate an uncovered park, holding 360 vehicles over hourly or daily periods.

CAR HIRE. Hertz and Avis have staff and car fleets at the airport.

TELEPHONES. Two banks of booths can be found in the main concourse and there is a booth in the buffet.

BANKING. The Royal Bank of Scotland operates a mobile branch at the airport, offering services which include issuing and accepting travellers cheques and foreign currencies.

SHOPPING. The shop close by the buffet stocks most items sought by the air traveller, including cosmetics and first aid products.

EATING. A licensed restaurant provides a grill and griddle service from 11 a.m. to 10 p.m. Monday to Friday and on Sunday, and from 11 a.m. to 9.30 p.m. on Saturday. A buffet is open from 7 a.m. to 11 p.m., Monday to Friday, 7 a.m. to 9.30 p.m. on Saturday and 8 a.m. to 11 p.m. on Sunday.

A bar, now being doubled in size, is open during the normal licensing hours applying in Scotland.

Getting to and from the Airport

The airport terminal stands on the A.9 trunk route, adjacent to the M.8 motorway to Glasgow and the west, and two miles from the start of the M-way system between Edinburgh and Perth.

BY CAR

Take the A.8 or A.9 routes to and from the centre of the city, using the Glasgow Road and the Queensferry Road respectively.

BY TAXI

Taxis are available at the airport terminal entrance and those on the stances in the city centre will carry any passenger requesting transport to the airport. A recommended price list to destinations is displayed in the terminal building.

BY COACH

Edinburgh Corporation's coach service carries passengers to and from the city terminal at Waverley Bridge, adjacent to the railway station at the east end of Princes St., linking with scheduled flights. A public bus service, operated by Scottish Omnibuses, passes the airport terminal at half-hourly intervals during most of the day.

BY RAIL

Nearest rail terminal to Edinburgh Airport is Waverley Station, Edinburgh, a major junction with services to all parts of Scotland and England.

During the 1972–73 period, when several minor improvements were made, aimed at easing pressure, passenger traffic rose by 14 per cent (with the main growth coming from domestic scheduled passengers). In aircraft movements, although domestic charters showed a six-fold rise, the 13 per cent increase in scheduled services represented five times as many passengers. Cargo and mail showed a combined increase of 46 per cent. Edinburgh's traffic continued to grow despite the oil crisis of 1973, and benefited from a rail strike in January 1974.

A significant development was the introduction by British Caledonian on 1 April 1972 of a nightly, walk-on 'Moonjet' service at half the price of the normal daytime fare. The service left Edinburgh and Gatwick at 11 p.m. and used BAC 1–11s. The airline also introduced a scheduled weekday service to Copenhagen via Newcastle on 1 November 1972, also using BAC 1–11s. They also introduced computerised booking facilities at their check-in desks on 1 February 1972.

One interesting point regarding the cost of the redevelopment of Edinburgh was that three quarters of the total cost was to be met by the Department of Trade, with the balance coming from the BAA. This was subject to a defined limit and was agreed under the terms of the transfer of the airport to the BAA. This was in contrast to the usual BAA practice of undertaking the cost of all major projects internally. The start of construction work on the new terminal was deferred by six months to meet a government directive to reduce capital expenditure in 1974/75. The total cost of the new terminal, runway and taxiways was £13 million at 1973 prices. Once again, with this delay and the pressure of passenger numbers increasing, a further expansion of the public concourse area was made in March 1974, increasing the total area from 1,620sq.m to 2,180sq.m to try and ease the pressure.

Work began in March 1975 on the new terminal building and, with the acquisition of Aberdeen and Glasgow Airports by BAA, a new division was formed, entitled 'Scottish Airports', including Prestwick and Edinburgh. It was to be based at Glasgow to control the activities of the Scottish airports. The view of BAA at this time was that the three Lowland airports would have overcapacity to serve the Lowland region whereas Aberdeen needed to be upgraded to cope with the increase in North Sea related traffic. By historical accident the Lowlands had three airports capable of handling three times their throughput of 3.4 million passengers (1976 figures) although this situation would change substantially in years to come. To be fair to BAA, although they felt there was a large overcapacity in Scottish airports, they embarked during this period on a new terminal and runway for Edinburgh, a new terminal with associated apron and taxiways for Aberdeen, and an extension for the Glasgow Airport terminal, which brought all these airports up to a decent standard. A policy statement was issued in relation to the Lowland airports by which Prestwick was to serve the needs of long haul intercontinental traffic while Edinburgh and Glasgow were to cater for short and medium haul flights. Glasgow was to serve the centre and West of Scotland and Edinburgh the Eastern region.

During this time, BA decided to rearrange, replacing their Viscounts on Scottish routes in the summer of 1975 with two HS 748s.

Edinburgh Airport had mixed fortunes in the recession following the oil crisis. It made a loss of £191,000 (itself following from a £108,000 loss the previous year) which grew to £213,000 the following year. In addition to this, BAA's capital programme was affected by inflation in the construction industry at 22.5 per cent during 1974/75 and they were forced to borrow government money for the first time in seven years. There was a fall in domestic traffic at Edinburgh of 6.8 per cent although there was a temporary surge in traffic by the end of 1975 due to the closure of Glasgow Airport because of a municipal workers strike. Further industrial troubles at other airports in March 1975 showed the total inadequacy of the terminal when 5,000 passengers passed through in one day. This was twice the norm for that time of year. Equally there were a high number of diversions from Edinburgh in January and February of that year due to crosswinds.

To give some idea of how badly crosswinds affected the main runway 13/31, causing diversions to other airports, it is useful to compare Edinburgh to the other BAA airports in 1975/76, showing the number of hours the main runway of each airport was affected by cross winds greater than 20 knots:

Heathrow (runway 10/28)	31 hrs
Gatwick (runway 08/26)	6 hrs
Stansted (runway 05/23)	23 hrs
Glasgow (runway 06/24)	29 hrs
Edinburgh (runway 13/31)	122 hrs
Prestwick (runway 13/31)	91 hrs
Aberdeen (runway 17/35)	46 hrs

A total of 28,455 passengers were affected by diversions from Edinburgh in 1975. It was a wholly unsatisfactory state of affairs, and deeply frustrating for the passengers. Significantly, the first year of operation of the new runway 07/25 saw the number of hours of crosswind greater than 20 knots drop to 7 hours from the 122 hours mentioned above.

By 1976 Edinburgh was recovering from the worldwide recession, and there was a 5 per cent increase in passengers and an 11 per cent increase in air transport movements. This was offset by a 42 per cent decrease in cargo handled, although this was largely due to the suspension of a nightly newspaper flight which accounted for approximately half of Edinburgh's cargo traffic. There was a general decline within the UK of short haul cargo traffic in any event.

Edinburgh was the first of the Scottish airports to introduce a domestic sound-proofing grants scheme on 1 April 1976, similar to those operated at Heathrow and Gatwick.

For anyone sitting on the left-hand side of an aircraft landing on runway 13, this would have been the view. This picture was taken from Viscount G–AOHV on 23 June 1973 on flight No.BE8192 from Glasgow to Edinburgh. (Alexander J. Cunningham)

The new runway and taxiway were completed and ready for operations on 1 April 1976, along with a new fire station and motor transport unit. A total of £80,000 was spent at the same time on the start of a landscaping programme to screen the airport activities and protect the surrounding areas. One unusual feature of the new facilities was the placing of two 'Archimedes screws' at the end of the apron which took drained water from the runway to be passed into the Gogarburn, the water being at a lower level than the 'Burn'. The Gogarburn itself feeds into the river Almond.

Due to industrial action by firemen, the new runway was not used for seven days after it was officially ready for business, finally opening on 7 April. This industrial action was a protest against the restrictions imposed by BAA on transatlantic flights, which had to use Prestwick instead of operating directly to Edinburgh. It was estimated that 90–95 per cent of tourists to Scotland included Edinburgh in their schedules, so it was safe to assume that a high proportion of passengers would prefer to go straight to Edinburgh rather than Prestwick. Wardair had already carried out a survey which showed that 80 per cent of the respondents wanted to go direct to Edinburgh. Also, in anticipation of the new runway opening, the American airline Capitol International Airways had already organised a charter flight with 250 passengers booked to fly from Minneapolis to Edinburgh for a seven day holiday in October 1977 using their 'stretched' DC8–61. When landing permission at Edinburgh was refused they cancelled the entire trip at an estimated cost to the local Edinburgh economy of £50,000. The industrial action had the backing of the TGWU (Transport & General Workers Union) who felt that a change

Overhead shot of airport just after the opening of the new facilities. (Colin Lourie)

BA Trident landing on runway 31 – in a typical crosswind. The new terminal takes shape in the background. (Colin Lourie)

to the arrangements would mean the creation of new jobs due to the increased traffic. The protest was also against the initial decision not to allow 24-hour operation of the airport (opening hours were restricted to 08.00–24.00) as this would also have created up to a possible twenty-five new jobs for the BAA, with further positions being created by the airlines. The restricted opening hours also meant that tour operators Cosmos, Brighter Holidays, Globespan International and British Caledonian all had to trim their Inclusive Tour programmes to fit in with airport opening hours. The first aircraft to use the new runway was a BA Trident landing from Heathrow.

The new runway had full Cat. II status for lights and ILS, but one shortcoming of the runway was the absence of a full-length parallel taxiway, something which was not to be rectified until nearly thirty years later. Noise from aircraft using the new runway was a prime consideration. In addition to the sound-proofing grants scheme (previously mentioned), an offer was made to buy the twenty-two cottages most affected at Lochend, Newbridge, under the Land Compensation Act (Scotland). It was also decided to maintain the existing night-time closure of the airport.

The longer runway meant larger aircraft and aircraft with greater payloads could operate from Edinburgh, and this allowed the introduction of a far more comprehensive holiday charter programme with flights to a number of new destinations but primarily to the major holiday spots in the Mediterranean. Prior to this, passengers had had to travel to connect with holiday flights from Glasgow and the London airports like Gatwick and Luton for holiday charters.

The new terminal was officially opened by Her Majesty the Queen on 27 May 1977, and it became operational on 29 May 1977. Covering an area of 146,000sq.ft, it was designed initially to handle 1.5 million passengers per year. The terminal offered three airbridges (a first for Edinburgh), gates for ten aircraft, and a full range of catering facilities, shops, check-in desks, immigration facilities and all the paraphernalia of a proper international airport. One feature of the new terminal was that it had been designed to make the average distance from the terminal forecourt to the aircraft door around 50m. It was a vast improvement on the previous facilities, and the general view was that Edinburgh now had an airport to match its status as Scotland's capital. The terminal building had been designed to allow ease of expansion and, with the opening of the new terminal, the numbers passing through the airport continued to grow; terminal passengers increased by 22 per cent from 853,000 to 1,042,000, air transport movements increased by 11.5 per cent from 18,400 to 20,500, passengers traveling on the airport's main route to and from Heathrow increased by 27 per cent from 448,000 to 567,000, international charter passengers increased from 21,000 to 73,000 and, finally, as a result of the new runway, the number of passengers diverted to other airports was negligible, compared to the 23,000 passengers diverted in the previous year. The one dark spot among these improved figures was cargo, which declined by 30 per cent. Despite this decline in cargo there was considerable interest shown in a scheme to convert the old passenger terminal for cargo operations when passenger operations were transferred to the new terminal building.

Germanair A300. This was the first of the new 'widebody' aircraft to visit Edinburgh. (Colin Lourie)

BA Trident 1 G–ARPR, July 1980. This Trident went to Teesside Airport on 16 September 1981 for fire service training at the end of its flying days. (Robert Pittuck)

As early as 1973, BA/BEA had started to introduce the Trident in place of the Vanguard on the Heathrow route. The major growth over the following years (and the largest in actual passenger numbers) had been on this route as a result of the introduction by British Airways in April 1976 of a new concept (from the USA) of a shuttle service on their three major UK routes – Heathrow to Glasgow, Edinburgh and Belfast. It was based on the idea that anyone who had bought a ticket got a guaranteed seat, and back-up aircraft were used at busy times when the initial aircraft was full to capacity. It turned out to be a great success and passenger numbers continued to grow on all the shuttle routes.

Another successful service, which was to run throughout the 1980s, was a direct Edinburgh–Tingwall (Shetlands) service, operated by Loganair using Twin Otters. The service started on 2 April 1979 with Twin Otter G–RBLA. The airfield at Tingwall was more convenient for Lerwick than the airport at Sumburgh.

Turnhouse had never received scheduled transatlantic flights as government policy had designated Prestwick as the gateway airport for flights to and from Scotland. When the new runway and terminal became operational, Wardair of Canada, Canadian Pacific, Transair Canada and the national carrier Air Canada had all expressed an interest in operating flights from Edinburgh but, due to the use of Prestwick for transatlantic flights, none of them could do so. The Viscount service (as previously mentioned) was still being flown from Aberdeen to Edinburgh and Prestwick to connect with the Prestwick transatlantic services. Later, this service was taken over by Loganair using a Short SD330 aircraft. The service was subsidised by the BAA and, in the 1979 season (July to November 1979), the service carried 4,000 passengers. However, in the following 1980 summer season this 'Translink feeder service' carried far fewer passengers. The inadequate demand was through no fault of the carrier but it resulted in a loss to Loganair and an unacceptably high subsidy per passenger to the BAA. It was therefore reluctantly decided that the service would be discontinued.

Loganair Shorts 360, parked at the 'old terminal' area when it was being brought into service as the cargo area. (Colin Lourie)

When Edinburgh still only had its old 13/31 runway it was unable to deal with the larger aircraft on the services to North America, and the use of Prestwick for these flights was necessary. However, once the construction of new facilities had been completed at Edinburgh, there was dissatisfaction in many quarters that these flights still had to go through Prestwick. Two Pan-American Boeing 707s actually landed at Edinburgh shortly after the opening of the new runway but this was an exception as they were a one-off charter as opposed to a scheduled service. This matter was of concern to the Edinburgh Airport consultative committee on the opening of the new facilities, as they felt that the full potential of the airport were not being utilised. They argued that there should be some easing of the restrictions for long-haul flights. They put their views in a memorandum which was forwarded to all relevant parties, including the fourteen MPs representing the constituencies served by the airport. The committee, along with local MPs, made strong representations to the Secretary of State for Scotland to amend legislation regarding the banning of sale of liquor on Sundays, so that liquor could be sold at the airport throughout the whole week. This amendment was agreed upon, and liquor sales on Sunday began in October 1977. The committee was also instrumental in persuading HM Customs & Excise to allow duty-free facilities. An agreement on this issue was reached in time for the opening of the new terminal. The only other problem that concerned the committee was the heavy road traffic generated by the Royal Highland Show at Ingliston Showground, although assurances were given that airport traffic would have priority over the showground traffic.

A Britannia Airways Boeing 737 discharging passengers. (Colin Lourie)

As mentioned previously (Norman & Dawbarn suggestion for a rail link at Gosford), the possibility of a rail link to the airport by re-opening the old Turnhouse Halt on the main line to the north from Edinburgh was investigated. Talks were held with British Rail, but it was eventually decided that there would be insufficient traffic to warrant the re-opening of this stop.

The policy setting out traffic patterns for the three Lowlands airports was reaffirmed in a government statement on 19 December 1979 (which maintained the status quo) issued after a meeting between government ministers at the Scottish Office and Department of Trade and the chairmen and representatives of the BAA and British Airways. After the meeting the Department of Trade issued this statement:

> The BAA reaffirmed that the most economic proposition for the foreseeable future is to continue operating all three airports as complements to each other and to reach financial breakeven, that in their view this represents the most effective use of the airports, and that they have no intention of applying to the Secretary of State for Trade for his consent to the closure of Prestwick. The two ministers concurred in this view.

There were parties within the aviation industry that felt that Prestwick existed to the detriment of Edinburgh and Glasgow airports, forcing long-haul traffic (transatlantic flights in particular) to go to Prestwick when in many cases they wished to go direct to Edinburgh or Glasgow. The problem was that Prestwick's original role as the first point for aircraft to land and refuel after the long transatlantic crossing had now been superseded with the advent of longer-range aircraft. During the 1979–1980 period, the BAA-operated coach service between Edinburgh city centre (with a stop at Edinburgh airport as an added facility) and Prestwick was increased to two coaches per day (from 9 April 1979) in each direction in an attempt to improve inter-airport connections in the Lowlands. Timings were geared for early morning passengers travelling to Edinburgh. About 12,000 passengers had used the service to 31 March 1980.

In 1980, Loganair took over the Belfast to Edinburgh route from British Airways and later started flights to Manchester as business traffic started to represent an increasing share of its passengers.

Edinburgh's trading results improved considerably by 1980, and the deficit was reduced to only £16,000. From a financial point of view the whole of the 1980s was spent driving towards break-even (agreed with the government on 26 February 1980), not just for Edinburgh but for the Scottish Airports division as a whole. Investment in facilities that year alone at Edinburgh was £3 million. This was set against a backdrop of increasing passenger traffic with only Spanish charter traffic showing a decline. This was more than offset by the new direct flight charter destinations. The choice and frequency of routes from Edinburgh improved, with a new direct scheduled service to Kirkwall, an upgraded service to Lerwick and improved weekend services to Birmingham. Inter City Airlines began a service to Brussels via East Midlands airport. Air UK added additional flights to their Edinburgh–Leeds and Edinburgh–Amsterdam services in addition to their Aberdeen and Humberside services using F.27s and F.28s. Additionally, the summer

Air Anglia F.27. (Colin Lourie)

services to Jersey and the Isle of Man which had originally been dropped as uneconomical were restarted. Charter traffic increased by 41 per cent to 147,000 in 1981/82 and this prompted an extension of the international departure area, costing £400,000, in order to cope with the increased figures. The total charter destinations now included Alicante, Barcelona, Bucharest, Constanta, Gerona, Ibiza, Malaga, Milan, Munster, Munich, Palma, Pula (Yugoslavia), Rimini and Tenerife, flown by airlines such as Britannia (Boeing 737), Aviaco (DC8 & DC9), Dan Air (Boeing 727), Monarch (Boeing 737 & BAC 1–11 – they had phased out the Boeing 720 by the early 1980s), JAT (DC9), Sterling (Caravelle), Nor-Fly (Convair 440 and 580), Braathens (Boeing 737), Linjeflyg (F.28) and Altair (Caravelle). The 1979–80 period also saw the use of larger aircraft for the first time on charter flights, such as Laker Airways DC10s and A300s. A British Airways L1011 Tristar was used on the busiest day in February 1980 to take passengers on scheduled flights from Heathrow for the Scotland–France rugby international. Around 7,000 passengers used the airport that day. Two other 'firsts' during this period were the largest number of passengers to use the airport in one month (140,000 on July 1979) and the first visit of Concorde to Edinburgh on 23 March 1980. Thousands of people came to the airport to see her. She turned out to be an Air France Concorde (F–BVFC). It was three more years before the first British Airways Concorde came to Edinburgh, when G–BOAF arrived on 29 November 1983. A further rugby 'highlight' came on 22 March 1982 when a Boeing 747 arrived with a full complement of French rugby supporters and was turned around to depart with 400 holidaymakers in 90 minutes. The summer of 1982 saw twenty-five tour operators (eight of them using Edinburgh for the first time) offering holiday tour flights to twenty-one holiday destinations.

Aer Lingus Boeing 747, not a normal visitor, being associated mainly with rugby charters. (Colin Lourie)

Improvements were made within the terminal, including duty-free facilities for travellers to the Irish Republic, and an extension to the shuttle gate room. The period from the opening of the new terminal up to 1980 was one of sustained progress. However, cargo showed another decline (7 per cent). New cargo facilities were in the process of being built, and this was to bring about a great change in the number of flights and cargo handled. The number of cargo flights had actually increased despite the overall decline, due to the use of smaller aircraft.

The BAC 1–11 was still a regular visitor to the airport, being used by British Caledonian on their Gatwick service and by BA to Manchester and Birmingham. Smaller aircraft were also starting to be used on scheduled services during the early 1980s, including Business Air's Gulfstream G1, Air Ecosse's E110 and Loganair's fleet of Trislanders, DHC6, ATP, and their Short SD330 and 360.

The continuing drive by the BAA for self-sufficiency for the three Lowland airports was given a boost by an increase of 35 per cent in landing fees (applicable from 1 April 1980) on top of a 15 per cent increase only five months previously, along with rigorous cost-control measures.

The early 1980s was a period of slight decline in passenger numbers, although this was reflected elsewhere due to the worldwide recession. Despite this, however, inclusive tour operators offered direct flights to Greece and Austria for the first time in 1980. Other developments in the airport included the improvements to gates 5 and 6 to improve passenger flow, and an extension to the duty-free shop. BP and Esso officially opened

Boeing 727 of the Yugoslavian charter operator Aviogenex. (Colin Lourie)

their new fuel terminals adjacent to the main apron in December 1980 and February 1981 respectively. The most important item on the airfield itself was the upgrading of the main runway to Category III status in December 1980, enabling aircraft to operate in low visibility conditions.

Air Ecosse also introduced new scheduled services to Aberdeen and Liverpool for passengers, plus new direct mail flights between Edinburgh, Aberdeen, Luton, Liverpool and East Midlands. This was under contract to the Royal Mail and was in addition to the British Caledonian Gatwick Mail service. This was a major contract aimed at ensuring that mail posted at the end of the day would be delivered the following morning throughout the various provincial centres. There was an extension to the night-time opening hours to allow for these flights and initially there was a certain amount of uneasiness about the noise levels from the additional flights. However, demonstrations by Air Ecosse with the Bandeirante turbo-prop aircraft allayed fears after the noise levels were monitored at the most environmentally sensitive points.

There was also pressure in the early 1980s from the tour operators study group, which demanded that the airport should allow night-time flights, or at least to extend the opening hours. Their view was that this would allow more economical use of aircraft, leading to cheaper package fares and therefore more traffic. This was taken into account, but the view of the BAA and Airport Consultative Committee was that the effect on the environment and the hardship caused to residents in Newbridge and Cramond would be too much and that it was better to await the advent of quieter aircraft expected to come into service by 1986.

Overhead view, looking from the south-west. (Glenn Surtees)

Tunisair Boeing 737, British Caledonian BAC 1-11 and BA Viscount,. The Archimedes screws are visible in the background. (Colin Lourie)

An early view of stands 1 to 4. An Aer Lingus Fokker 50 is pushed back on stand 9. (Gordon Sandford)

Another early view, before the apron expansion. (Gordon Sandford)

Alidair (now renamed Inter City Airlines) introduced a new scheduled service to East Midlands, and Loganair introduced a new Kirkwall service as well as increasing the daily frequency of its flights to Belfast.

There was good news for the BAA accountants at this time, as the rateable value of the airport was reduced by more than half. On appeal the Lands Valuation Appeals Court reduced the rate from £1.1 million to £500,000.

One shortcoming of the new runway was the absence of a full-length parallel taxiway, which meant that aircraft had to backtrack on the runway at both ends. BAA obviously recognised this and, in their capital expenditure programme for 1981/82–1985/86 they had allowed a sum to be set aside for the extension of the taxiway to the end of runway 25. The sum was 2.7 million in 1980/81, £3 million in 1981/82 and 3 million in 1982/83 (along with £1 million for an apron extension). However, the taxiway never materialised until over twenty years later. The BAA report for 1985/86 stated that the taxiway extensions would only be built 'if justified by changes in the mix of aircraft'.

On 13 May 1981, in response to a parliamentary question, the Secretary of State for Trade, Mr John Biffen, stated (amongst other items relating to aviation policy) that it was still official policy that Prestwick would act as the long-haul gateway airport, but that there would be a relaxation of the rules so that Edinburgh could handle a restricted number of transatlantic charter services related to the Edinburgh Festival and other local requirements. This appeared to be the first slight change in Edinburgh's traditional role as a purely short- and medium-haul airport serving the Eastern Region.

The short length of runway 26 presents no problem for this Royal Navy Sea Harrier. It is landing after a display at the Rosyth Navy Day. The picture was taken before the Falklands campaign. (Gordon Sandford)

In 1982 a House of Commons Scottish Affairs Committee, chaired by the MP for Central Ayrshire, looked at aviation in Scotland. One of its suggestions was that there should be a Scottish Airports authority under the Secretary of State for Scotland. This suggestion was condemned by the BAA who stated that their Scottish Airports division was autonomous, and defended their record, pointing out that £50 million had already been invested in the Scottish Airports, with a further £40 million planned for the next five years, most of it generated by internal BAA funding without recourse to public money. The BAA also pointed out that it would be for Parliament to approve any change of ownership in Scotland's airports. The formal government response published on 2 March 1982 expressed similar views to those held by the BAA and again confirmed the status quo of the positions of the three Lowland airports.

Despite the statement by John Biffen regarding relaxing long-haul restrictions, British Airtours, in 1982, made and then withdrew an application to operate series charters on an Edinburgh–Belfast–Toronto route. The apparent reason for the withdrawal of the application was that there was insufficient public support for these charters, but it was felt that the proposal was still in conflict with the BAA policy of transatlantic aircraft using Prestwick. At the time BAA reassured the airport consultative committee and other relevant parties that aircraft which made a transit through Prestwick to Edinburgh would be subject to a rebated landing fee in order to make the proposition more attractive. This position was formalised in a memorandum issued by the Scottish Office on 2 March 1983 regarding stopover flights. It did, however, require an amendment to the Air Service agreements with the USA and Canada as, under the licensing agreement in place at the time, a carrier could make a transit stop at Prestwick before proceeding to an English or foreign airport but could not take passengers to and from another Scottish airport.

This period also saw the launch of the 'Scottish Take-Off' marketing campaign, aimed at developing maximum support from the holiday trade (including airlines) for existing holiday charter services. The initiative began with a presentation to travel agents and tour operators and included a booklet listing every inclusive tour destination from Scotland. Travel agents were also supplied with posters, window display material and other point-of-sale items. The campaign was based on the premise that a significant proportion of Scottish-originating holidaymakers travel elsewhere to catch their overseas flights and were unaware of the direct services available from airports in Scotland. Much of the promotional effort was aimed at helping Prestwick, but all Scottish airports benefited, including Edinburgh.

The 1982/83 season saw mixed results. There was further growth on the Heathrow route, a 40 per cent increase (over the previous two years) on the Loganair service to Belfast (a route taken over from BA) which was mainly due to the shift of its operation from Aldergrove to Belfast Harbour Airport from 21 November 1983. There were increases in the summer charter passenger numbers plus a strong mail-carrying programme with sixty movements a week, carrying 8,000 tonnes of mail per year. Airport improvements included the start of a £500,000 redevelopment to the Shuttle Lounge plus the opening of an extension to the duty-free facilities and tax-free shop. Against this, Inter City Airlines had to withdraw the Brussels service (which had been

A scene reminiscent of the 1950s. Instone Airlines Bristol Freighter G–AMLK lands on runway 31, early 1980s. (Gordon Sandford)

introduced in March 1982) due to inadequate demand. There also appeared to be weak demand for winter holiday programmes.

One of the most distinguished passengers to pass through Edinburgh Airport was his Holiness Pope John Paul II, who arrived on 31 May 1982 and departed on 2 June 1982. A second 'Scottish Take-Off' campaign was mounted in the winter of 1983, along with a BAA-sponsored 'Gateway Mission' in October of that year to Canada. This involved the Scottish Tourist Board and other Scottish tourism-related organizations visiting cities and other locations to make presentations and direct sales with the primary aim of encouraging inbound tourism through Prestwick, but with a hope that the promotion would also benefit other Scottish airports such as Edinburgh. The second 'Take-Off' campaign was carried out mainly through TV advertising, and was aimed at persuading local holidaymakers to fly from their local Scottish airports. Market research after this campaign showed it to have been particularly successful, with more public awareness of the choices available.

The period from 1983–1984 saw expansion in all areas for the airport as the worst of the recession appeared to be over. Passenger figures exceeded 1 million for the first time in the year to December from March (the BAA year runs from 1 April to 31 March). Total income rose by 27 per cent, domestic traffic rose by 9 per cent, air transport movements rose by 13.4 per cent, the service to Paris was reintroduced in January 1984 on a weekday basis by Air Anglia (it had previously been discontinued in 1980/81 through lack of support) and licence applications were made by Aerotime (trading as Scottish Executive Airways) for routes from Edinburgh to Copenhagen, Brussels, Frankfurt and also Paris (in addition to the Air Anglia service). Air Ecosse took over the

Air UK Bae 146 – the photograph was taken when the Spectator Terrace was open. (Glenn Surtees)

Aviogenex Boeing 737. In common with many airlines of former Communist countries, Aviogenex switched to Western-made aircraft from Russian models like the Tupolev Tu–134, previously operated by them. (Glenn Surtees)

Aer Lingus Shorts 360 EI–BEW. Since their first flight with a DC3, Aer Lingus have used virtually every aircraft type they have flown on their Edinburgh service (including rugby charters). (Glenn Surtees)

East Midlands–Edinburgh–Aberdeen route following the collapse of Inter City Airlines, with the same timings and frequencies, using Short 330s and 360s. It had been operating the route on a temporary basis following the collapse of Inter City but was granted the licence to permanently operate the route. European charter traffic rose by 18 per cent, with Moscow and Leningrad being added for the first time, the services being operated by the Soviet airline Aeroflot.

Perhaps one of the most significant events with regard to the effects on passenger numbers and services from Edinburgh was the application by British Midland Airways to compete against British Airways between Edinburgh and Heathrow. Up until 1983 British Airways (and their forerunner BEA) had a monopoly on the route (apart from a brief period in the early 1960s when the short-lived British Eagle service also offered the route). It had long been regarded as the preserve of BEA and then of BA. British Midland had originally applied to the CAA in 1981 to serve Edinburgh and Glasgow but were denied permission. However, they appealed to the Secretary of State, and he overturned the CAA decision. BMA were then granted permission to operate a service in direct competition with BA on these major UK routes, later to include Belfast. It is interesting to note that, at a meeting of the Edinburgh Airport consultative committee prior to the granting of the licence to operate, the overall view was to support BMA's application but that there were 'serious reservations' and 'one outright objection' expressed. The reservations centred mainly on the possibility that over-provision of capacity on the route might lead to all services becoming uneconomical, eventually resulting in reduced services and increased costs, to the ultimate detriment of the customer. In the event the total opposite turned out to be the case. Once BMA started flying, the knock-on effect was large increases in passenger numbers, increases in services by both airlines and a reduction in fares. BMA started the service to Edinburgh on 7 March 1983 using DC9–15s on a five flights a day schedule to BA's eleven daily return flights using Trident IIIs with Trident IIs as back-up aircraft. BA started to withdraw the Tridents and replace them with the new Boeing 757–200 from the beginning of February 1983, which was a much quieter aircraft with passenger appeal. The fierce competition between the two airlines on the Heathrow route offered passengers a choice of 180 movements per week, a figure that was later to rise.

BMA made a number of improvements to gate 1 (their London departure gate), flight catering standards improved, as the two airlines engaged in the 'Breakfast Battle', and BA introduced their 'Super Shuttle' concept on 30 August 1983, which was an improved service. The figures on the Heathrow route showed a 20 per cent increase in traffic in the last seven months of the financial year, with this route accounting for 56 per cent of all passenger traffic through Edinburgh, offering over 200 movements a week on this route alone. BMA still held a 28 per cent market share on the route by the end of 1983 despite a 2–4 per cent drop from the summer figures after the launch of the BA 'Super Shuttle'. BMA were also constrained by a lack of capacity as their DC9–15s were frequently full, causing passengers to be passed on to BA. Two DC9–30s were acquired by BMA to relieve the situation. Part of BA's shuttle concept was the guarantee that if an aircraft was full, any extra passengers were guaranteed a flight by having a back-up aircraft ready. If there was only one extra passenger, he would therefore have the whole aircraft to himself. This formed the basis of a television advertising campaign by the airline in 1983 which showed one passenger flying in style after his shuttle flight was full. Questions were asked as to how many times this had actually happened. The answer was once. The cost of providing a back-up aircraft for a single passenger (who

USAF Lockheed C.141 Starlifter. (Colin Lourie)

had paid £56 for his ticket) was £10,000. In order not to get into trouble with the Advertising Standards Authority, BA were expected to have provided this service at least once in the previous year, which they had. BA had, however, provided scores of back-up aircraft, and on many occasions only a handful of passengers were carried in the second aircraft. At other times when for technical reasons a back-up aircraft was not available, the passengers were passed on to British Midland with a £5.50 refund voucher because the British Midland service was cheaper.

British Midland were to later replace the DC9s with a mix of new Boeing 737s (300/400/500 series) and the odd flight by Fokker 100s. The competition between the airlines, along with the shuttle concept, has provided a great boost to Edinburgh which continues to this day.

Despite a slight drop in international passengers and cargo figures, mail throughput increased once again by 9 per cent to 9,000 tonnes. In addition to the above, Globespan, in conjunction with Worldways of Canada, reported the introduction of a new weekly service using a DC8 between Edinburgh, Prestwick and Toronto to start in June 1984 and end in September. This was a highly significant development as it now opened up the way for transatlantic services into Edinburgh on a regular basis even though the flights were routed through Prestwick instead of the previous arrangement of transatlantic flights having to be linked to specific events in Edinburgh or the surrounding region. BA confirmed a new scheduled year-round service linking Edinburgh with Aberdeen, Orkney and Shetland in addition to a new summer service to Jersey. Air UK started a new scheduled service to Stansted from April which linked Edinburgh for the first time with all three major London airports.

Air France Boeing 747 parked on ORP area at the end of runway 30. (Colin Lourie)

USAF Boeing C–135. (Colin Lourie)

March 1984 brought another rugby 'high' when 10,000 international passengers passed through for deciding matches against Ireland in Dublin and France at Murrayfield. Other unusual visitors were Concorde, which operated scheduled flights to and from Heathrow on St Andrew's Day (30 November 1983), and a USAF C–5A Galaxy, the world's largest aircraft, with an all up weight of 364 tonnes, which arrived to pick up a mini-rescue submarine and its crew in September 1983. The loading of the submarine took place towards the end of runway 13 where the Galaxy had parked facing down the runway. One of the new generation of 'quiet' jets, the Bae 146, was based at the airport in January 1984 during very severe winter weather conditions, in order to carry out snow and slush trials.

Despite the number of applications to fly to new European destinations direct from Edinburgh in the mid–1980s, an origin and destination survey carried out earlier by the CAA showed that, in 1982, a total of 24,000 passengers had flown from Edinburgh to Paris via Heathrow, 82,000 passengers had flown to other Continental destinations via Heathrow, and 12,000 passengers had flown to the Continent from Edinburgh via Gatwick.

Edinburgh moved into a trading profit for the first time in 1984/85 as did the whole of the Scottish Airports division of BAA, achieving the targets set by BAA. The total profit of the group was £4.4 million, set against the base year loss of £3.3 million in 1982/83. Edinburgh showed a profit of £900,000 against a loss of £1.1 million the previous year. Only Prestwick continued to show a loss. One particularly good piece of news was that the year-on-year decline in cargo traffic at Edinburgh was reversed, with a 4.4 per cent increase. A small but encouraging development at the time. However, an application for Freeport status for Edinburgh Airport was rejected.

Apart from a halt in international charter traffic, the mid–1980s again showed large increases in all areas. The slowing of the holiday charter traffic was mainly due to a significant number of passengers opting to go through, and travel from, Glasgow Airport which, for a number of destinations, generally had lower fares due to operating larger aircraft. Despite this, there was the largest gain for eight years in passenger numbers, which were up by 16 per cent to 1.5 million, plus a large 17 per cent increase in ATMs (Air Transport Movements), to 34,600. Four Airlines operated over 270 movements a week between Edinburgh and Heathrow, Gatwick and Stansted. The Heathrow route again showed very strong growth – 20 per cent – due to the BMA/BA rivalry.

Following on from the attempts to promote direct Continental flights, there was an increase in the frequency of services to Amsterdam, Paris, Dusseldorf and Frankfurt. Aerotime applied for licences to operate direct flights to Brussels, Frankfurt, Milan and Copenhagen using the new SAAB Fairchild 340. Air UK also started a new daily weekday service to Copenhagen via Newcastle (a service operated briefly by British United Airways some twenty years previously). Edinburgh Airport staff also took part in two promotional campaigns during the year in Paris and Amsterdam which were to encourage more visitors to Scotland and especially to Edinburgh. These campaigns were organized by the Scottish airports in conjunction with the major UK operator on the route, and also included representatives from Edinburgh city tourist group.

VIP visitors during 1984 included the Soviet premier Mikhail Gorbachev. Cardinal Glemp of Poland passed through.

Loganair leased BAC 1–11 G–AZUK from Ryanair Europe to provide extra capacity in 1989. Aircraft pictured 9 July 1989. (Iain Hutchison)

US Marine Corps A4 Skyhawk, stationed at Turnhouse during an exercise. (Colin Lourie)

In the on-going saga of all long-haul traffic for Scotland going to Prestwick as the designated airport, there was a significant point made in the long-term BAA Corporate Plan issued in March 1985. The plan reinforced the policy of using Prestwick for long haul and Glasgow and Edinburgh for medium/short haul but, for the first time, the policy view reflected the following statement by the Secretary of State for Transport, the Rt Hon. Nicholas Ridley MP: 'If however, a change in the fortunes of Prestwick does not come about by 1989, the decision to maintain the existing policy will have to be reconsidered' (Hansard, 4 April 1985, col.740). This statement was made at the end of a longer policy statement proposing privatisation of the airport group and expressing concern at the declining traffic figures at Prestwick.

This was recognition that factors such as the failure of efforts to promote Prestwick, the lack of success in the feeder services, and the losses being sustained by the airport, were forcing a rethink in policy.

Also in Parliament around this time, Richard Page MP asked the Secretary of State for Transport what percentage of passengers travelling to Heathrow and Gatwick from the major regional airports had transferred on to international flights. For Edinburgh the percentages were surprisingly high (Hansard, 7 March 1985, col.582):

Edinburgh–Heathrow: 864,000 passengers – 40 per cent transferred from/to international flights

Edinburgh–Gatwick: 152,000 Passengers – 31 per cent transferred from/to international flights

The exceptional traffic growth of 1984/85 levelled off in 1985/86. Increased prices in the inclusive tour market were one reason for this, along with a decline in the popularity of certain Spanish holiday destinations which had always been popular with Scots holidaymakers. The decline in the international Inclusive Tour market from Edinburgh was 22 per cent, but this was offset partly by continued domestic growth of 6 per cent, and the airport showed a healthy current cost operating profit of £1.1 million. The international Inclusive Tour decline was reflected across all UK airports, not just Edinburgh. BA added an extra round-trip service to their Heathrow schedule from the summer of 1986. During the year BA, BMA, Air UK and British Caledonian operated a total of 15,167 flights to the three main London airports. BMA kept up the pressure on BA with the introduction in 1986 of their one class international business service (Diamond Class) which was introduced on their five main routes from Heathrow including Edinburgh.

There was still uncertainty over the international scheduled routes, however, and Air UK had to withdraw from the Edinburgh to Paris service at the end of February 1986. However, on 26 October 1986, Air France started a Paris–Edinburgh–Aberdeen service with the first flight undertaken by Boeing 737-200 F-GBYB. In 1987, some of these flights were undertaken by TAT F28s. Air UK were able to move up to larger equipment (BAC 1–11) on the route to Amsterdam due to healthy passenger numbers. For the third season running Globespan operated a Worldways DC8 on the route to Toronto via Prestwick.

New noise regulations came into force in January 1986, and resulted in BA gradually phasing out the noisy Trident towards the end of 1985, to have all services operated by the environmentally friendly Boeing 757-200. Back-up for the BA 757s (previously provided by Trident IIs) was now undertaken by hush-kitted BAC 1–11s, which were also used by British Caledonian on the Edinburgh–Gatwick route.

The 1980s saw Aer Lingus using different aircraft on its service to Dublin. These included the Shorts 360 and Fokker 50 (a reminder of the old Friendship services in the early 1960s).

The speed record set by Squadron Leader Topp in August 1956 was broken on 1 July 1987 by two RAF F4J Phantoms of 74 Squadron (celebrating the seventieth anniversary of the squadron). Cliff Spink, flying ZE361, coded 'P', set a new record at 27 minutes and 3 seconds. Steve Smith was in the rear seat. Phantom ZE360, coded 'O', flown by Ian Gale, was a few seconds slower. The rear seat of ZE360 was occupied by Ned Kelly (whose birthday it was that day). The F4J model of the Phantom had been bought secondhand from the USA (actually from the giant storage facility at Davis Monthan Air Force Base in Arizona) and had General Electric engines as opposed to the ear-splitting Rolls Royce Speys of other RAF Phantoms.

There was a three-fold rise in cargo traffic in 1986/87 but this was mainly due to Glasgow night-time cargo traffic being diverted to Edinburgh whilst the runway was being resurfaced there.

The British Airports Authority became a private company in 1987, being floated on the stock exchange with a capitalisation of £1,225 million. Edinburgh became a wholly owned subsidiary called Edinburgh Airport Ltd within the group. The airport

Captured between the spans of the Forth Road Bridge, a BA Boeing 737 lands on runway 25. (Gordon Sandford)

continued to show strong growth in international and domestic sectors at the end of the 1980s and the operating profit grew to £2.3 million. A new domestic check-in and baggage reclaim area was added in May 1988 and the apron by the main terminal was extended to the east to allow more flexible parking for aircraft. The extension allowed for either two Boeing 737-sized aircraft or one widebody up to DC10 size. In 1988 Air UK, who had taken over the Gatwick route from British Caledonian, introduced the Bae 146 on the route in October of that year, and the number of passengers using the service showed a considerable increase compared with the figures from BCal's time.

The 2 million passenger mark was broken for the first time in 1988/89. Also in January 1989 the BAA asked the government for the first time to reconsider the positions of both Glasgow and Edinburgh in relation to receiving direct long-haul traffic. They stated quite clearly in the 1989 BAA report that 'it was clear to the board that Prestwick had not established itself with the Scottish air traveller or the airline industry as Scotland's intercontinental airport. Furthermore, Glasgow and Edinburgh are the only major UK regional airports which are prohibited from handling long-haul traffic'. It was misinterpreted as a call to close Prestwick but the government response through the Secretary of State was to decide against a review and wait to see what effect improved surface access had first.

May 1989 also saw Edinburgh becoming a 24-hour airport for the first time. This was trialled during the summer season, and tour operators responded by increasing the number of holiday destinations available. The 24-hour opening led to a 12.5 per cent increase in domestic travel and a 23 per cent increase in inclusive tour traffic (against a national pattern of decline in this traffic) to an overall total of 2.4 million passengers for 1989/90. These figures were reflected in a 23.2 per cent increase in revenue for the airport and an increased operating profit of £6.7 million. The British Midland gate area was enlarged due to strong growth on their routes and their use of larger aircraft.

9
1990 to the Present Day

Finally, after years of uncertainty, the major event of 1990 was the decision on 6 March 1990 by the Secretary of State for Transport to allow an 'Open Skies' policy, allowing airlines free choice to fly to any of the three Lowland airports which best suited the passenger market – subject to the terms of international air service agreements. This was in response to a legal challenge by the charter airline Air 2000 in May 1989 which questioned Prestwick's role as the sole gateway airport.

Glasgow appeared to be the greatest beneficiary of the relaxation of the rules, as the US and Canadian scheduled operators moved their services there from Prestwick in May 1990. However, the important point was that there were now no restrictions, and Edinburgh doubled its transatlantic passenger numbers in the first year after the relaxation. The 'Open Skies' policy was, needless to say, welcomed by the BAA. The first Gulf War saw a general decline in passenger numbers in the UK, although flight frequencies to Stansted were doubled. Edinburgh was also nominated as a major new hub for Royal Mail first-class post. A two-year runway resurfacing programme was completed in 1991 at a cost of £3.8 million, and there was further investment in a new main runway fire hydrant system to provide additional water supplies for the airport fire service in the event of an emergency. There were also further extensions to gate lounges, and an additional aircraft stand was constructed.

The recession in the very early 1990s caused a slight drop in domestic traffic (which accounted for 80 per cent of Edinburgh's passengers) along with a drop in charter traffic due to the trouble in Yugoslavia. Despite this, however, an upgrade programme costing £5 million was set in motion, which would include a new gateroom, built for BA's domestic passengers, the doubling in size of the international baggage reclaim hall, and the enlargement of the arrivals concourse area. The gateroom facilities for Belfast passengers were also upgraded and a new air jetty was installed along with an enlargement to the terminal building frontage (airside) to cater for larger numbers of passengers in larger aircraft. A new direct service to Southampton was also added, a service which had once been operated in the late 1960s via Glasgow by BUA with a Viscount.

One long-awaited improvement was an airport hotel, which was built near the airport approach road by Stakis Plc with 138 bedrooms, and opened in early 1995. It is only 200 yards from the terminal building.

US Marine Corps C–130. (Gordon Sandford)

Fuji Film Airship, G–BIHN. The original 1950s terminal building is in the background. (Gordon Sandford)

Easyjet started a three-times-daily service to Edinburgh from Luton at the end of 1995 after the success of their Glasgow marketing campaign, offering to fly people to Scotland for the price of a pair of jeans (£29 one way). They have gone from strength to strength and are now a major operator at Edinburgh. Sabena improved its service to Edinburgh by dedicating their twice-daily Bae 146 service direct to Edinburgh. Previously the service was to both Edinburgh and Glasgow. Glasgow received its own twice-daily direct service at the same time. In effect, Sabena had doubled its Scottish services from 26 March 1995. Aer Lingus operated SAAB 340Bs and the Bae 146 to Dublin, eventually settling on the Airbus A321, which now plies the route.

The year 1995 saw the failure of Macair, the Edinburgh based Jetstream 31 operator. The airline ceased operations on 26 June 1995 after being in existence for only two months. The airline had been using two Jetstreams, leased from Sun Air of Scandinavia, on a pattern linking Edinburgh and Birmingham with Carrickfinn and Londonderry. Further plans to fly from Derry to Stansted were stopped by the introduction of Jersey European's low fare, through plane services between the two points via its Belfast City hub. The failure of the airline was partly blamed on the bankruptcy of its sales agency (Total Mobility of Ware, Herts) which carried out all reservations and ticketing for the airline. However, it was felt that the experiences of Macair and Genesis Airways (which had ceased efforts to fly a low-cost service from its base to Belfast City one month before Macair's collapse) suggested that the Jetstream was not the best aircraft to tackle a competitive and low yield market like Northern Ireland.

Despite the failure of Macair, other airlines were having some success; BAC Express started a Liverpool–Edinburgh–Liverpool service with an F.27–500 in July 1996 and established a number of bases (including Edinburgh) in January 1999. BAC Express now undertake contract passenger and freight work including carrying mail for the post office. American Trans Air operated a series of summer charter flights from June 1995 to 1998 with Boeing 757s to New York, but there was still no scheduled service up until Continental started. SAS also started a new Stockholm service in 1996, with DC9-41 OY-KGB operating the first flight.

The mid–1990s also saw the demolition of the original 1950s terminal building. It was replaced by a new cargo development costing £3.2 million. This provided a total of 32,300sq.ft (3,000sq.m) of transit accommodation and freight forwarders buildings, with associated car and lorry parking and service areas with a one-way traffic management system.

One sad event occurred on 26 February 1996, when the old Trident G–ARPL used for fire training was cut up with a chainsaw for disposal. This aircraft had originally arrived at Edinburgh on 26 March 1982.

Another sad event was the official closure of Turnhouse as an RAF station on 25 March 1996. At the closing ceremony on that day, as the RAF ensign was lowered for the last time, there was a fly past by four Bulldog T1s of the ELUAS (Eastern Lowlands University Air Squadron) followed by three Gazelle AH1s. In attendance on the ground were an HS.125 (ZD703) and a Gazelle (XX456). A rather quiet end for a distinguished fighter station.

The Spitfire Gate Guardian at the entrance to RAF Turnhouse had originally been dedicated in a ceremony on 9 March 1957. The Spitfire itself (RW393) has been replaced by a replica and after the closure of RAF Turnhouse the replica was moved close to the entrance to the airport on land generously donated by the British Airports Authority.

1996. The sad end of Trident 1 G–ARPL, which had served many years with the airport fire service after its withdrawal from commercial service. (Colin Lourie)

Station Headquarters and entrance to RAF Turnhouse. (Squadron Leader Bruce Blanche Collection)

Old control tower. (Squadron Leader Bruce Blanche Collection)

Gazelle in front of RAF Buildings, Turnhouse. (Squadron Leader Bruce Blanche Collection)

It was re-dedicated in a ceremony on 27 October 1996. The original Spitfire RW 393 is now on display in the museum at RAF Cosford with the serial TB675.

Air UK transferred flights from Gatwick to London City Airport in 1996. BA then took over the Edinburgh–Gatwick service with Boeing 737s.

As for the old RAF facilities, they are currently being used as part of the airport's air cargo operations. There was a proposal that the facilities should be used to provide a reception centre for housing up to 750 asylum seekers while their applications were processed. However, these proposals have been shelved and it seems likely that the facilities will continue to be upgraded and used for air cargo or light industrial and office use.

Euroscot started a service to Bournemouth from Edinburgh in September 1997. This service proved successful with healthy load factors and was later operated by Gill Air. The airport won the *Executive Travel* magazine award in 1997 or Best Regional Airport, with Glasgow in third place, after London City Airport. Edinburgh was runner-up to Manchester in the 1996 awards. The awards are based on polls taken from the most frequent travellers and are based on year-round assessments.

Continued growth from the mid-1990s onwards (Edinburgh was now Scotland's fastest-growing airport) plus a large boost by low cost airlines opening up new routes and offering very low fares, meant the facilities were once again struggling to cope with the increased traffic and passenger numbers. £54 million was set aside in 1996/97 to extend and reshape the terminal building to provide new domestic facilities, a completely new centralised check-in hall with forty-six check-in desks offering greater capacity, improved retail facilities, a complete separation of arriving and departing international passengers, and a new international arrivals hall.

On the airside, two new air jetties were added, along with four new aircraft stands accommodating aircraft up to Boeing 757/767 size. The first phase of this major project opened in May 1999 and the rest of the completely remodelled terminal was opened in March 2001. The occasion was marked by a visit from Sarah Boyack MSP, Scotland's Transport Minister. A further 12,500sq.ft (1,200sq.m) of additional retail space was added to the terminal during this redevelopment. New shops in 1997/98 were Books etc., Sock Shop, The St Andrews Links Golf Shop and Thornton's. A significant portion of airport income in all BAA airports comes from retail concessionaires. The total redevelopment of the terminal had taken nearly five years and £100 million. The beginning of 1999 saw the closure of the spectators terrace which ran along the front of the main part of the terminal building. Many people mourned the loss of this excellent facility, but security issues are now paramount at many airports in the UK and abroad. Hopefully a time may come in the future when this will be reopened.

Runway 08/26 was closed on 11 July 1999. The last landing was Piper PA28 Archer (G–ANGT) at 18.15, flown by Bob Graham. The last take-off was a few minutes later, by a Cessna 310 of Edinburgh Air Charter. Development has now encroached on to this runway at the 08 end, in the form of additional car parking areas and General Aviation parking and offices.

On 1 October 1999, 603 squadron was reformed and given back its prestigious title of No.603 City of Edinburgh Squadron, taking on the role of No.2 MHU (Maritime

Headquarters Unit). This was basically a 're-role and re-badge' exercise, and its function now is entirely ground-based.

The summer of 1999 saw one of the most significant periods of expansion in international services from Edinburgh. There were new scheduled services to Basle by Crossair, Frankfurt by Lufthansa, Paris by BA (Air France also upgraded their Edinburgh–Paris schedule) and Vienna by Tyrolean Airways. In a ten-year period Edinburgh's passenger figures had grown from 1.8 million in 1987 to 4.6 million in 1997/98 with no sign of the growth abating. Numbers had actually doubled in the previous seven years. The opening of the new Scottish Parliament in Edinburgh was also expected to increase passenger throughput by as much as 350,000 passengers a year. The cargo and mail sectors also continued to grow. The 5-acre cargo village was the hub of TNT's Scottish operations, providing an integrated depot linking the carrier's road-based network to the airport's cargo operation. The cargo village is also a key centre for the Scottish operations of UPS, DHL and the Royal Mail, being the small parcels hub for Scotland. Titan Airways and Channel Express are also regular freight and mail carriers. New hardstandings were created by the old RAF area to provide additional parking for cargo aircraft in addition to the old main apron (from the 1950s and 1960s) which was now solely dedicated to cargo and mail operations. Cargo grew by 50 per cent in 2002 due to strong growth in the express parcels sector.

Loganair continued to be a strong user of Edinburgh. All Loganair aircraft now operate under a BA franchise (BA Express) and carry BA colours. Loganair is also affiliated to the Oneworld alliance (American Airlines, British Airways, Cathay Pacific and QANTAS). Sadly, tragedy befell one of their aircraft on 27 February 2001, when a Loganair Shorts 360 (G–BNMT), in BA colours under the franchise agreement, took off for Belfast on a chartered Royal Mail flight but went into a steep dive shortly after take-off and crashed into the Firth of Forth killing both crew members. Eyewitness reports stated that the aircraft had made an attempt to return to the airport after issuing a 'mayday' due to double engine failure, but it went on to crash 6 minutes after take-off.

Flyglobespan Boeing 737-683 G–CDKT. Flyglobespan have carved a niche for themselves in the low cost market, initially from their Scottish customer base. (Martin Krupka)

Sea Vixen in Red Bull colours. Based at Edinburgh for the weekend while performing at the Museum of Flight's annual flying display. (Colin Lourie)

The 6 million mark for passengers handled in a twelve-month period was passed in 2001/2002, largely due to strong growth on routes served by low cost carriers. This improvement was also against a generally depressed background in UK aviation and worldwide, particularly in the aftermath of the terrorist attacks on September 11. New low cost routes introduced included Easyjet to Gatwick and Belfast, GO to East Midlands and Bristol, Ryanair to Dublin and British Midland to Brussels. The following year further low cost routes were started to Cardiff and East Midlands by Bmibaby, the low cost arm of British Midland. New scheduled services to Cologne, Cork and the Isle of Man were started in 2002/2003.

Percentage growth was a very healthy 13.1 per cent, and passengers handled exceeded the 7 million mark. Four additional aircraft stands were constructed to ease parking at peak periods, and a multi-storey car park was also constructed at this time. The flood defences for the river Almond were improved as the amount of land development around the airport and to the west of the city had led to flood mitigation measures on the Gogar Burn.

Flyglobespan established bases at Glasgow and Edinburgh and launched flights in April 2002 from both airports using a mixture of Boeing 737 models. Although a low cost airline, it has aimed at flying to main airports rather than outlying airports and has carved a niche for itself serving a predominantly Scottish customer base.

D–AQUI – Ju 52 – operated sightseeing flights over the Edinburgh area. (Colin Lourie)

One of a number of German AF Mig 29s on a refuelling stop on their way to exercises in North America. (Colin Lourie)

In 2002/2003 a set of threshold limits for noise were agreed with Edinburgh City Council, and a Noise and Track monitoring system was installed so aircraft noise and approach routes could be precisely monitored in accordance with the limits.

A number of significant events took place at the airport in 2003. In March British Midland Regional introduced a daily Edinburgh–Jersey service after becoming one of the first airlines to receive funding from a Scottish Executive initiative to encourage new direct routes. Thirty years previously this route had been a Saturday service only during the summer months, operated by a BEA Viscount. This service was in addition to BMI Regional's Brussels–Edinburgh service which had been a success. The funding is a great help to the airport in securing new routes. The Scottish Parliament and Executive initially provided £60 million (since increased to £95 million) for a route development fund to aid Scottish airports in getting new routes up and running.

It was decided in August that, to accentuate the image of the city of Edinburgh as a major centre of the arts, the airport should be involved in the International Arts Festival in August 2003 by having a very small part of the festival take place on the airport concourse. It was a useful exercise, as many people fly to Edinburgh for the festival. The airport also featured in a 'one-off' episode of the BBC's *Airport* documentary series in November 2003. The episode was watched by an estimated 5 million viewers.

Work finally started in November 2003 on the extension of the parallel taxiway to both ends of the main runway. This had always been a shortcoming, as aircraft were

Concorde on its last visit, turning to taxi back down the runway, 24 October 2003. (Allen McLaughlin)

Concorde on its last visit, with the Scottish flag being flown from the cockpit, 24 October 2003. (Allen McLaughlin)

having to backtrack on the runway, causing delays at busy periods. The new taxiway extensions were completed in February 2004. The distinction of the first aircraft to 'use' them went to a Lithuanian TU 204 which was parked on the new taxiway leading to runway 6 for several days before the taxiway was officially opened for use.

One truly memorable occasion took place on 24 October 2003 when Concorde G–BOAE visited for the last time before being phased out of service. She visited a number of cities (Manchester, Belfast, Birmingham, Cardiff and Edinburgh) as a last farewell, starting from Heathrow on the 20 October and flying to each city in turn. When G–BOAE landed at Edinburgh, she taxied down the runway with the Scots flag flying from an open cockpit window before turning around and taking off, a magnificent and sad sight at the same time. The last Concorde flight (with selected BA staff) actually took place from Heathrow to Filton on 26 November 2003.

One of the Concordes (G–BOAA) is now on display at East Fortune museum. Another unusual visitor on 12 August 2002 was a Boeing 707–138B (N707JT) piloted by Hollywood film star John Travolta. The aircraft is painted in the old 1960s QANTAS 'V jet' livery, and stopped in Edinburgh during a round-the-world trip organised as part of a QANTAS marketing campaign. The aircraft itself was built and first registered in September 1964. The 'V Jet' livery was introduced in the early 1960s when QANTAS had taken delivery of the new 'B' version of the Boeing 707–138 aircraft and modified the rest of their fleet to this configuration, using the revolutionary turbo-fan engine. The 'V' in 'V jet' stood for the Latin word *vannus*, meaning fan. John Travolta is a qualified commercial pilot and it has been said that if he tires of his Hollywood job he can always fly commercial airliners for a living!

December 2003 saw the first scheduled flights from Edinburgh to Stockholm by SAS and Moscow by Transaero, although Moscow had been served as a holiday charter destination previously. The airport also opened on Christmas Day 2003 for the first time. A direct scheduled service to New York (Newark Airport) was started in June 2004 by the American airline Continental using Boeing 757s. The initial seven flights a week was increased to ten flights a week, which were timed, as much as possible, to connect with flights in the USA, Canada and Latin America. This was a long sought-after service and is expected to show healthy passenger numbers, especially during the summer months. A second USA destination will be served from 4 May 2006 when Delta Airlines will start their new service to Atlanta with B757s.

Edinburgh, unfortunately, missed out on a route to the Middle East starting in 2004. Emirates Airline had wanted to start a Dubai service from Scotland but selected Glasgow instead of Edinburgh as, although they felt Edinburgh would have more business passengers and a stronger traffic class mix, they favoured Glasgow on account of its slightly longer runway. Emirates were starting the operation with the A330–200 but have the intention of switching to the much larger Boeing 777–300 once traffic numbers start to grow. They were not prepared to operate from both airports and, as stated, the range and payload restrictions of Edinburgh's runway ruled out the possibility in any event. Instead,

An Aer Lingus A321 departs for Dublin while a BMI A321 taxis for its own departure to Heathrow. (James O'Sullivan)

New control tower and Spitfire Memorial. The current Spitfire is a replica of the original Spitfire RW393 which had been the personal aircraft of Air Marshall Sir William Elliot in 1949. (Squadron Leader Bruce Blanche Collection)

Ilyushin IL96 carrying President Vladimir Putin of Russia and his wife on their visit to Edinburgh, July 2003. (Colin Lourie)

Business-Class passengers within a 100-mile radius of Glasgow are offered free courtesy transport and first-class passengers are offered the same service with an unlimited radius.

Aer Lingus introduced the A321 in May 2005 on a three times a week basis to Dublin. The low cost operator Jet2.com started an Edinburgh–Manchester service and recently announced their intention to serve other destinations from Edinburgh including Edinburgh–Murcia in summer 2006 but the other destinations were not specified at this stage. Central Wings started a new Warsaw service on 31 October 2005 and Easyjet will serve Geneva from 15 December 2005. Other planned destinations to be served in 2006 include Finnair to Helsinki from 12 April 2006, BMI to Munich from 26 March 2006, Sterling European Airlines to Helsinki from 30 March 2006, and Sterling European Airlines to Stockholm (Arlanda) from 27 February 2006.

The latest cargo figures showed that there has been a great increase in the sector in the last thirty years or so. In 1969, when cargo was a very quiet affair, the total amount handled was 3,470 tonnes; it is now over 56,000 tonnes (including mail). As mentioned previously, Edinburgh is Scotland's hub for the Royal Mail's Skynet service (Skynet being the Royal Mail's integrated movement of mail by air) with flights going to Heathrow, Gatwick, Stansted, East Midlands Airport, Bristol (and onward to Bournemouth), Liverpool, Belfast, Aberdeen and Inverness. Inward flights to Edinburgh are also handled from all these airports. All Skynet services at Edinburgh are 'self handled, that is, the mail is delivered to the operational area of the airport by Royal Mail vans, where it is unloaded, segregated, and loaded into the aircraft by postal staff. They also carry out the handling for dedicated Parcel Force aircraft. Titan Airways have a dedicated Boeing 737-300 (G–ZAPV) in Royal Mail colours to take mail from Edinburgh to East Midlands Airport. The initial contract was for four months but has recently been extended to two years. In addition to the Skynet services, many scheduled passenger aircraft also carry mail in and out of Edinburgh on behalf of the Royal Mail, primarily to Birmingham and Norwich, but also to some of the airports previously mentioned. Up until the mid- to late 1980s, both Abbotsinch and Prestwick handled the majority of air cargo in Scotland. Nearly all the cargo throughput (approximately 90 per cent) at all Scottish airports was and still is actually sent via road to the main London airports. Manchester and East Midlands Airport (EMA) and incoming cargo is carried the same way. KLM actually truck air cargo through to Amsterdam from Scotland with consolidation at Manchester and the Midlands. This is mainly due not only to there being fewer services but also to the smaller aircraft sizes in operation from Scotland.

Today, Edinburgh Airport handles 8.4 million passengers annually (90 per cent on scheduled flights, 10 per cent on charter flights), 26,900 tonnes of cargo, 29,700 tonnes of mail, and 104,000 air transport movements. Over forty airlines fly to nearly sixty destinations with 3,600sq.m of retail space. There are forty-five check-in desks plus twelve self-service check-in kiosks in the terminal. The airport has thirty-one parking stands of various sizes, plus a further twelve dedicated stands for cargo operations. The airport also has one 2,760sq.m maintenance hangar along with three separate airline engineering workshops each with its own dedicated compound. A good indicator of the growth at Edinburgh is the main route to London. At the time of the 1967 Fettes College

Ilyushin IL62, supporting aircraft for Russian President Putin's visit, July 2003. (Colin Lourie)

survey there were sixty-six flights a week between the London airports (Heathrow and Gatwick) and Edinburgh. Today there are, on average, 200 flights a day on weekdays (1,200 flights a week) between Edinburgh and the London airports (Heathrow, Gatwick, Luton, Stansted and London City Airport) making this route (London–Edinburgh) the busiest in the UK.

In 2002, the Fraser of Allander Institute, one of Scotland's most respected think-tanks, estimated that the three Scottish BAA airports contribute some £1.5 billion to the Scottish economy and support as many as 32,000 jobs. With regard to Edinburgh, it was estimated that the airport supports over 8,000 jobs across Scotland and directly employs 3,200 people (400 are BAA). Direct employment at the airport is forecast to increase to 5,700 by 2013 and to 9,000 by 2030. The airport's contribution to the Scottish economy is estimated at nearly £300 million a year.

Recent developments have included a brand new multi-storey car park with space for 2,000 cars. It cost £20 million to build and was opened by Councillor Donald Anderson on 27 September 2004. Its design won the Best New Car Park award in the British Car Parking awards in March 2005.

Another major improvement was the construction (started in October 2003) of a new 57m-high control tower by the main terminal. The old tower was a rather ramshackle affair by the old RAF facilities and attached to a building, but served faithfully and was adequate for the job. As stated earlier, it had originally been the visual control room at Blackbushe airport before being relocated to Edinburgh to replace the old Second World War control tower. However, once the new terminal and runway were built, the whole airfield could not be physically observed from the old tower. There was a lengthy period before a decision was made on a new tower, and discussions with the National Air Traffic Control Service (NATS) about funding was the main issue. The new tower

Easyjet Boeing 737-36N G–IGOR. Easyjet are now a firmly established operator from Edinburgh. (James O'Sullivan)

View of the terminal taken from the new multi-storey car park. (James O'Sullivan)

Belgian Air Force ERJ145LR, serial CE–03. (James O'Sullivan)

cost £10 million and now dominates the skyline. Building work on the futuristic and impressive-looking tower was completed in the summer of 2005 and it became operational at 10.24 p.m. on 15 October 2005. The first aircraft to be handled by the new tower was a Gulfstream 5 from Dallas. The official opening of the tower took place on 7 November 2005, and it was opened by the Transport Minister, Alistair Darling. The use of the new tower will allow an increase in runway movements from thirty to thirty-eight an hour. The dramatic and eye-catching design of the tower has won the Commercial and Retail Project of the Year award at the Annual Builder and Engineer Awards held in November 2005.

The airport is almost becoming a victim of its own success, as delays at peak times are hampering both scheduled and charter services. Figures released in October 2005 showed Edinburgh only second to Gatwick in terms of delays suffered by passengers. However, new measures and investment in facilities (a new £14 million pier, rescheduling of runway slots plus the new control tower) are expected to alleviate the problems. A £2 million plan to transform the entrance to the airport was also started in November 2005 to ease congestion and improve traffic flow. The work will take five months.

Anne Follin, BAA's Planning and Development Manager for Edinburgh, has said that the aim of the British Airports Authority will be to transform the airport of today, which handles 8.4 million passengers per year, into one with the ability to handle 20 million.

10
The Future

The airport has benefited greatly from being in a good location on the 'right' side of Edinburgh (closer to the Central Scotland Belt as well as near to the Forth Bridge and main line railways and main roads to the West and North of Scotland). Glasgow's Abbotsinch Airport is on the Western side of Glasgow so anyone travelling from Central Scotland (for example, Falkirk or Stirling) has to pass through the city of Glasgow to reach it. Whilst Glasgow Airport has always had greater passenger numbers, Edinburgh, in the late 1990s and early part of the twenty-first century, has consistently shown greater percentage growth, and has been one of the fastest growing airports in the UK. It is expected that Edinburgh will overtake Glasgow in overall passenger numbers and air transport movements by 2015.

The proposed future of air transport was detailed in a Government White Paper announced in Parliament on 16 December 2003 by the Transport Minister Alistair Darling (a former Edinburgh councillor and Edinburgh resident). In the White Paper it was proposed that either Glasgow or Edinburgh airports be given a new runway to cope with the large projected increase in demand but it is now possible that both airports may get new runways. As mentioned previously, the possibility of a Central Scotland Airport (instead of Glasgow and Edinburgh) was again examined but dismissed. The new runway would be built parallel to, and west of, the current main 06/24 runway (06/24 is the re-designated 07/25). In addition to the runway capacity required for increased numbers, the terminal facilities will have to be expanded by two to three times the current size in order to cope.

The main railway line from Edinburgh to Fife and Aberdeen passes along the airport boundary, and for many years a possible rail link to the airport was suggested but always rejected on grounds of cost. Previous suggestions had focused on a station being built on the current line with a bus link to the terminal building. However, on 3 February 2004 plans were announced for a major project valued at £505 million to link the airport to the national rail network. Basically, it is proposed that two 1500m tunnels should be built under the main runway and the river Almond as part of the flagship project. A new low-level station will be built near the south-east corner of the airport terminal building. The two single-track tunnels will extend around 1500m from the terminal building under the runway and the river, before surfacing to the east of Carlowrie estate. The line will then split into two at Carlowrie, with one line going to Glasgow and the other to Fife, in effect allowing direct rail services to the airport from all over Scotland. Going eastwards from the terminal building the line will pass close to the existing Hilton Hotel before tunnelling under the A8 and rejoining the Edinburgh–Glasgow mainline near Ratho. Details of the scheme also included the confirmation of contractors to draft up designs before a private bill is lodged with the Scottish Parliament. Work on the project was expected to begin in 2006 with a tentative completion date of 2010.

Journey times on the main Edinburgh to Glasgow line will be unaffected, and it is hoped that trains will stop at the new airport station every 3 minutes, going to and from Edinburgh, Glasgow, Fife, Stirling, Aberdeen and Newcastle. The station would have the potential to handle ten trains an hour each way – four on the Glasgow–Edinburgh route, two from Fife, two from Stirling, one Aberdeen–Newcastle service and one from Inverness to Edinburgh.

There is no doubt that it is an expensive and complicated project; the managing director of the airport, Richard Jeffery, said, 'There is clearly a lot of work ahead to establish the technical feasibility of this proposal'. However, it should bring great benefits in terms of ease of travel to the airport from the rest of Scotland, which will increase passenger numbers and bring more jobs both on the project itself and as a spin-off of the greater usage of the airport. Other UK airports (Heathrow, Gatwick, Manchester, Southampton) have found rail links to the national network to be very beneficial. Richard Jeffery went on to say, 'However, BAA is committed to supporting these efforts in the months ahead. Progress towards the construction of the rail link is important in terms of the wider need to deliver an integrated transport policy for West Edinburgh, bringing together rail, trams – which we also support – and new and improved roads'.

It was also announced by Michael Howell, Chief Executive of Transport Initiatives Edinburgh, that Scott, Wilson & Halcrow had been awarded the engineering contract to develop the rail link design. The contract, worth £1.2 million, is jointly funded by BAA and the Scottish Office. Funding for the main part of the project has yet to be secured and that will be contingent on a good business case being put forward with the design, but all parties concerned are confident that this will not prove to be an obstacle. The proposed siting of the rail tunnel will involve the relocation of the *Cat Stane,* a 4ft-high stone believed to be over 1,000 years old and which marks the resting place of Vetta, an ancient tribal princess.

It is many years since the city of Edinburgh last saw trams but, in addition to the rail link, it is also planned for the airport to have a tram link. The new proposals are for two tram routes. The first is a circular one from Princess Street taking in Granton and Leith and the second is to go from Haymarket westwards with stops at Murrayfield Stadium, the Gyle Centre, Edinburgh Airport and the Royal Highland Showground. The line to the airport will be a spur line rather than a stop which will avoid the need for the line to pass through the Royal Highland Showground and also land that might be required for future airport expansion. There is also a suggestion for this tram line to run no further than the airport. It is estimated that the line will carry 4.2 million passengers and cost £230 million – £93 million more than the sum set aside for both lines by the Scottish Parliament. Barring any obstacles it is hoped to have the service running by 2009. There is still uncertainty over the tram proposal for the city, with funding being a major issue.

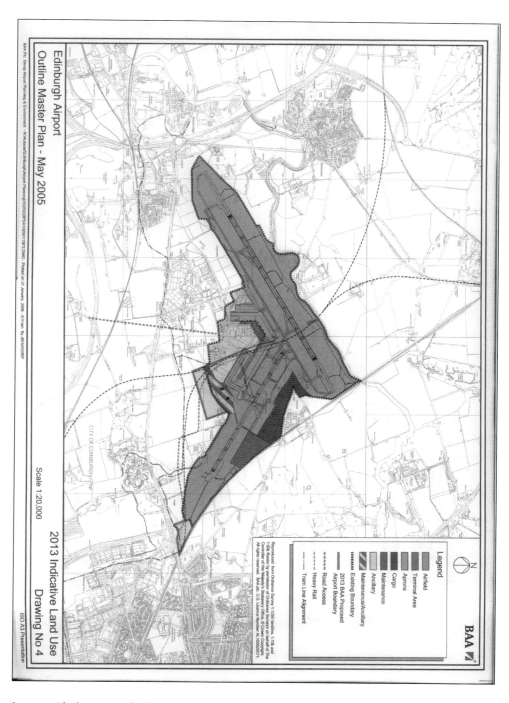

Reproduced from Ordnance Survey 1:1250 landline, 1:10k and 1:50k Raster by permission of Ordnance Surveys on behalf of The Controller of Her Majesty's Stationery Office, © Crown Copyright. All rights reserved. BAA plc. O.S. Licence Number AL 100020071.

Edinburgh Airport
Outline Master Plan – May 2005

Scale 1:20,000

2013 Indicative Land Use
Drawing No 4

Layout with the proposed changes for Edinburgh Airport in 2013. (BAA)

155

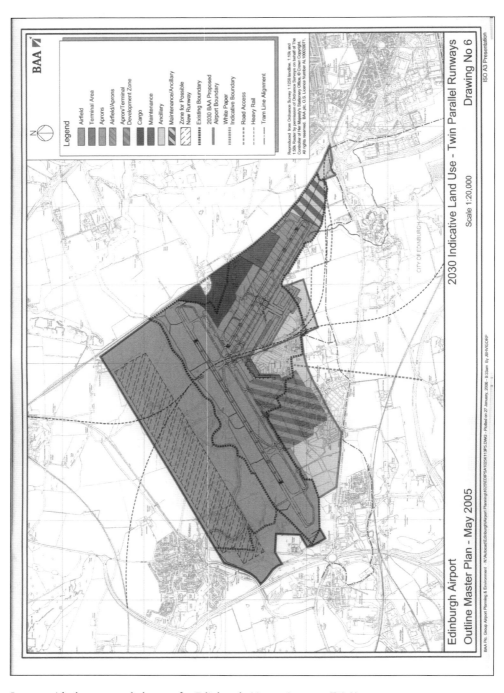

Layout with the proposed changes for Edinburgh Airport in 2030. (BAA)

The Outline Master Plan for Edinburgh Airport was released by the BAA in October 2005. The plan recognises the importance of the airport to the Scottish economy and looks at the proposed development in two timeframes – between now and 2013 and between 2013 and 2030, which is the upper limit of the timescale set out in the Government White Paper.

The forecasts between 2005 and 2013 are that passenger numbers are expected to grow from 8.4 million to between 12 million and 13.7 million. Aircraft movements are expected to grow from 104,000 per year today to between 138,300 and nearly 160,000. Runway movements are expected to grow from thirty-three per hour now, to between forty-two and forty-four per hour. Aircraft parking stands required will increase from twenty-nine now to between thirty-seven and forty-five. Cargo and mail tonnage is expected to grow from 56,000 tonnes to 71,500.

In the terminal building, more check-in desks, baggage reclaim, departure lounge and boarding gate facilities will be needed to meet the increased demand. The first stage of this, a new pier (costing £14 million) to serve the south-east apron from the terminal is already under construction and is expected to open in summer 2006. Two new maintenance hangars are likely to be required and finally the current 'on-airport' parking capacity of 6,200 could rise to between 9,500 and 10,500. New roads to cope with the increased traffic will also be required in addition to the surface links previously mentioned.

The period from 2013 to 2030 is less clear as it is further ahead, but it is expected that passenger numbers could grow to a top estimate of 26 million a year, air transport movements could grow to between 175,000 and 241,900, runway movements could grow to between fifty-eight and sixty-five, aircraft parking stands could grow to between fifty-eight and sixty-nine and finally cargo and mail could grow to 106,500 tonnes per year. Improvements to both runways (for example, high-speed turn-offs and greater use of runway 12/30) will be made to allow an increase in hourly runway movements from the current thirty-three per hour to fifty-five. Runway 12/30 is the re-designated old main 13/31 runway.

Overall, this would mean a further 10 hectares of land being required for cargo facilities in two stages up to 2030. For increased terminal and apron capacity, 34 hectares of land will be required by 2020 and a further 54 hectares would be required by 2030. The total of 88 hectares would all be required on land currently occupied by the Royal Highland Agricultural Society of Scotland. For the large increase in aircraft movements a second parallel runway will also be needed and 280 hectares of land north of the existing boundary will be required by 2030. There is also a proposal (should the need be required by the airlines) to extend the 06/24 runway from its current 2,560m to allow for a take-off run of around 3,000m. Any runway to be built north of 06/24 would have to take into account the river Almond, and the proposed alignment of the runway has not been fixed. On top of this, environmental factors would have to be taken into consideration.

The plan also stated that future growth at the airport was largely expected to be in international passengers and long-haul traffic and although domestic traffic is still expected to grow, it will be as a lesser proportion of overall traffic (70 per cent by 2013 and 50 per cent by 2030).

11
The Ferranti Flying Unit

By Len Houston (FFU Chief Test Pilot 1964–73)

In 1942, Ferranti Ltd, Edinburgh, now BAE SYSTEMS, was rapidly organised and built to manufacture the MkIIc Gyro Gun Sight designed by the Royal Aircraft Establishment and successfully continued to carry out this effort until the end of the Second World War, producing a total of 9,594 sights. The end of the war brought about a drop in demand, and it became evident that if business was to continue in Edinburgh, it was essential the company found ways to diversify its products.

Thus were laid the foundations of the future. During the course of events, the Ferranti Flying Unit was formed at Turnhouse and a fleet of thirty-four widely differing aircraft passed through the programmes, flown by nearly as many evaluation test pilots, fifteen of whom were employed by the company, including four navigators and a multitude of flight test engineers. Trials were conducted which led directly to equipping the RAF Lightning, Britain's first single-seat supersonic fighter interceptor, with the Airborne Intercept Radar and Pilot Attack Sight System, (AIRPASS AI23) and the later AI23B Head Down version; the Royal Navy Buccaneer Blue Parrot Strike Radar; Inertial Navigation and Attack System (INAS) into the Harrier and Phantom; and the Laser Ranger and Marked Target Seeker (LRMTS) for the Harrier and Jaguar. The world's foremost terrain-following radar system (TFR) also completed its full development and even extended the envelope. However, the political cancellation of the ill-fated TSR2 prevented the entry of that radar into operational service. Other projects interspersed within the major tasks ran in parallel throughout the years, and a later project to equip the Eurofighter with the ECR90 radar from 1993 to 2004, momentarily energised the FFU some twenty-four years after it was officially dismantled in 1969.

The company thus achieved the virtual monopoly on British expertise in military weapon-aiming systems, airborne interception and terrain-following radar, laser systems and navigation systems, all of which were principally flight-developed from Turnhouse. In the beginning in 1949, the civil aviation industry and the ministry identified the need for the development of an improved navigation aid, Distance Measuring Equipment (DME), and thus the first aircraft, Dakota Mk3 (TS423, ex-436 Squadron Royal Canadian Air Force), was allotted to the company for this project on 15 August

Framed by the tail of Gloster Meteor NF.11 WD790, a Buccaneer is prepared for flight. The nose of WD790 is now preserved at the North East Aviation Museum, Sunderland. (Len Houston)

Opposite above: Blackburn Buccaneer XK487 cockpit. This Buccaneer was the second prototype, fitted with Gyron Junior engines, which were very short on power, requiring take-offs with BLC (Boundary Layer Control). Extreme care was required for approach with BLC, and a minimum of 1000ft above the ground was required in the event of engine failure. (Len Houston)

Opposite below: Canberra LRMTS. (Len Houston)

Dakota departure. (Len Houston)

Dakota TS423 farewell. The tall man is Flight Engineer Stewart Watts. This picture was taken before TS423 went to Elliott's at Rochester for Head Up Display (HUD) work. (Len Houston)

Five serviceable aircraft. Chief Aircraft Engineer Tom McIlwraith was pleased to have all aircraft serviced for flying on this day only for a poor weather forecast to cause the cancellation of the planned flights. (Len Houston)

1949. Scottish Aviation Ltd at Prestwick were contracted to install the experimental equipment, maintain and fly the aircraft at Turnhouse, the project costs being funded by DA Arm, the ministry branch responsible. This aircraft was destined to remain on the fleet inventory until October 1967, completing eighteen years' development service for the company.

A two-seater Sea Fury T20 (VX301) arrived to carry out tests to evaluate improvements to weapon aiming with the same support arrangements, and it was at this crucial time that the joint Ministry of Defence and industry contract policy of utilising ministry trials aircraft was to be initiated at Ferranti. On 28 August 1952 an operation and maintenance contract began, placed solely with Ferranti, thus establishing the FFU as a definitive section of the company at Turnhouse, and with it the Trials and Installation Department (TID) at Crewe Toll, the location of the company's Edinburgh headquarters.

Trials for the development of a Royal Navy carrier-borne aircraft bad weather recovery radar then commenced at a site at Tantallon Castle, with ten to twelve Sea Hawk and Sea Fury aircraft provided by the Royal Navy from Lossiemouth added to the accumulating data and analysis being undertaken in temporary premises above Tattons the Jewellers in Rose Street, Edinburgh.

The trials had, by 1953, raised the fleet to five aircraft, now including the Fairey Gannet GR17 and a Valetta, for gunsight and bombing system tests respectively, with three pilots and a group of test observers crewing them. The first accident to the fleet occurred about this time when the pilot inadvertently retracted the Sea Fury landing gear after landing, and the flight test engineer accelerated at high speed from the aircraft clutching the valuable data recorded on the flight. The pilot left the company unannounced the next month, disappearing without trace.

Scottish Aviation at Prestwick were sub-contracted to complete a nose-cone installation in the Dakota, representing the engine intake radar 'pod' in the new Lightning P1B fighter, leading the breakthrough in the development of weapons systems technology by the Ferranti-led trials. In the same year, 1953, a fatal accident occurred on 26 September when the Sea Fury crashed whilst carrying out low-level aerobatics near Longniddry. The crew of two were lost. A similar aircraft replacement eventually came on to the contract. The fatal accident was the only one the FFU suffered during some thirty-five years of frequently hazardous flight-testing.

The number and types of aircraft allocated to Ferranti increased as the projects advanced, due in no small part to the requirement to operate target aircraft for specialised equipment tests. In addition, the bombing range facilities at Royal Aircraft Establishment West Freugh became a regular base. A Meteor (G–ARCX), purchased from English Electric, became the preferred 'taxi' to shuttle air and ground crews to and from Turnhouse, and the Dakota used rather less often to position the pilot and

Lightning Cockpit (XG312). The Radar Display Visor was made for the pilot to press his face against it to exclude daylight and was made of a very stiff type of rubber which was forced back if ejection occurred. (Len Houston)

Lightning XG312 with author of FFU section, Len Houston, waiting impatiently in pressure suit and Taylor helmet to depart on a high altitude flight. (Len Houston)

flight test engineer to the aircraft based at West Freugh, with no other occupants on board. Clearly consolidation of facilities was required at Turnhouse and a large wartime Type 2 hangar found at a disused airfield (Hethel, in Norfolk) was dismantled, transported to Edinburgh and re-erected there in May 1956 on the south side of the airfield. It was backed by a 60ft high, long, unbuttressed wall but was no sooner built than a high wind the following night caused it to collapse outwards, fortunately causing no damage to aircraft or personnel. The new arrangement eventually consisted of air and ground crew offices, laboratories and secretarial staff, drawing office and trials analysis support facilities and a *cordon bleu* canteen.

Canberra and Meteor aircraft of varying marks entered the inventory as the pace of development flying intensified. Included was Canberra B8 VX185 which started life as a B2, but converted to the prototype B5 version. Originally entered by the English Electric Company into the Trans-Atlantic race competition in which jet aircraft were at that time energetically engaged, it briefly held the speed record for the both-way same-day crossing. After converting into its final form as the prototype B8, it remained with Ferranti, operating as a target aircraft.

Managers assembled a team of aircraft inspectors and engineers with demanding responsibilities to ensure serviceable aircraft became available when the projects required them. As the fleet increased with its variety of different types – and many were early models of the type, carrying special technical modifications from their previous owners – only a highly competent and motivated staff could meet this unique challenge. Pilots and maintenance crews at the FFU established a bond of trust which served to remove any concerns that might have arisen over the safety standards in the fleet. That the company safely accomplished such prolonged success throughout testing is a tribute due to the maintenance personnel.

FFU Meteor, Canberra, Dakota. (Len Houston)

Gloster Meteor G–ARCX. Now at the Museum of Flight at East Fortune. (Len Houston)

The AI23 radar trials required higher performance aircraft testing, and a Hunter MkIV day-fighter equipped with an Echo Radar Ranging MkI feeding signals to the Light Fighter Sight paralleled the radar project with Canberra B8 WJ643 and WT327, both now fitted out with the Lightning radar. Other projects also ran throughout the years.

RAF Turnhouse, as it was then named, had no ground control approach radar and the FFU awaited the higher-performance, shorter-range Buccaneer second development aircraft fitted with the early Gyron Junior engines and no additional fuel tanks. The bomb-bay contained special equipment built in 'Forth Bridge style'.

To safeguard the aircraft which Ferranti were operating to carry critical secret military equipment, the decision was taken to install a Decca Approach Control Radar, ACR 7, on the airfield operated by Ferranti staff air traffic controllers co-located with the RAF controllers in the tower. This equipment now permitted flying to lower weather limits and, with the installation of a SafeLand Barrier at each end of runway 31/13 which followed when the prototype Buccaneer entered the trials, there was an immediate increase in the level of operational safety. The barrier was required only on one occasion when, during an approach by one of the Canberras in poor weather, the controller lost radio contact with it on finals but shortly reconnected. Meanwhile, the pilot who had commenced an overshoot at close range and still in cloud, quickly decided to lose height and regain the glideslope – by now too fast! Aquaplaning on the very wet runway surface, the aircraft engaged the barrier at a low speed and damage was limited to minor skin defects.

Two Canberras by the hangar doors. (Len Houston)

WV787 Canberra landing on runway 13. FFU pilots regularly made extremely low approaches, just missing the top of the airfield boundary. (Colin Lourie)

By 1959 the AI23 radar was being prepared for the next phase, installation in its intended final aircraft the Lightning P1B, and planning commenced which included a critical decision concerning the location of the airfield where the tests would be conducted. In keeping with the company policy of locating the aircraft in close proximity to the technical facilities and staff, Turnhouse was the first choice of the company. However, during a Lightning approach check, not including landing, by an English Electric (later British Aircraft Corporation) test pilot, the decision was taken against Turnhouse, based on the 'presence of the gasometer close to the runway centre line'. In fact, the correct decision had been made for another reason: the restricted runway length. When the trials took place over the next five years at Warton, your writer, now appointed the company's project test pilot and based at Warton, experienced a braking tail-chute failure on landing. Its runway was 2,000ft longer than the main Turnhouse runway at the time (6,000ft), and the aircraft was brought to a stop just before running off at the end! Later further justification for the decision arose during the demanding fuel-critical phases of the attack computer development. Head-on runs were flown with Aberporth Range control, at mach 1.7, 35,000ft, against a Lightning target, flying at mach 1.7 at 45,000ft, a 2,440mph closing speed. After accelerating the aircraft to the supersonic test speed over South Wales to complete the interception over the middle of Cardigan Bay, the attack signal on the head-down display demanded a pull-up towards the calculated weapon release. At this point the escape manoeuvre, inverting the aircraft 180 degrees and pulling 'g' to stop the climb, ensured safe separation from the target now passing overhead. Fuel was minimal as a result of the prolonged use of afterburner and had to be carefully conserved for recovery to Warton. Only one attack could be made with the fuel available.

Dakota TS423 received the first experimental model of the Terrain Following Radar and played an important role in the determination of appropriate low-level test routes before they were cleared for use by Canberra B8 WT327 and the Buccaneer XK487. It soon became apparent the severe rising ground in the Scottish Highlands selected for the tests challenged the Dakota's climb performance, and steeply banked turns away before reaching the high mountain peaks often occurred, until that part of testing was judiciously left to the jets!

Ferranti decided that the dispersal of test pilots and aircraft between Turnhouse and Warton and West Freugh, just two of the airfields utilised, required a swift means to locate the pilots with the project aircraft and so Meteor NF14 WM261, a two-seater night-fighter, was regularly brought into that role. Registered in the civilian category as G–ARCX, it now rests in the Museum of Flight at East Fortune, East Lothian. Painted in a white basic colour, with a red stripe from nose to tail identifying it as 'the Hexachlorophene tooth-paste with the stripe', it also served as an invaluable vehicle for the purpose of refreshing the essential piloting skills needed in the demanding task of maintaining low flying techniques on the routes and basic continuation training.

Hawker Sea Fury VX301 with pilot A.E. Featherstone and flight engineer Peter Gibson. This Sea Fury suffered major damage during a landing and was not replaced by the unit. (Len Houston)

DH Dove. This aircraft was not assigned to the FFU but was used by Ferranti for civilian purposes. It is seen here having come down in a field at Wester Hailes after a planned one-engine failure after take-off from Turnhouse did not go according to plan. (Colin Lourie)

Much test-flying, with the exception, of course, of the single-seat fighters, was crewed by the flight test engineers, most of whom had never previously experienced crew member duties, and the Dakota flying laboratory was often the first time for many. All aircrew received an initial course at RAF Mountbatten and the Royal Aircraft Establishment, Farnborough, in emergency training, including pressure chamber decompression, survival equipment, dinghy drill, sea survival and helicopter winching rescue and, in some cases, ejection seat training. Regular re-approval courses were also carried out through an agreement with RAF Leuchars Air Sea Rescue Squadrons. Flights often extended to 5 hours or more in the Dakota, compared with some 50 minutes of high-speed, very low-level work in the Buccaneer, and high altitude, supersonic in the Lightning. Crew seating in the Canberras provided only an ejection seat for the pilot, but the method of abandoning the aircraft in emergency for the two engineers was through the entrance door. The time taken to effect such an exit was recorded in the hangar at Turnhouse (with an inflated, upturned multi-seat dinghy to land on); the test engineers took only 4.5 seconds to complete the task! Great credit is deserved by them. The pilots had full confidence in their remarkable ability to handle the flight check lists and test schedules and to adapt to often physically uncomfortable, demanding and, at times, stressful conditions.

These systems engineers also possessed a detailed knowledge of the equipment, often boarding the aircraft having just completed repairs or adjustments in the lab or the flight line. As an example, the Forward Looking Radar trials had reached the stage when a

100ft selected clearance height outside the original specification was to be examined. The radar design engineer was offered the rear seat. Having agreed, an immediate aircrew course was scheduled. He quickly acclimatised to his new role and, on his return, experienced his first flight at the system's lowest ground clearance of 100ft, at an airspeed of over 500 knots, and some of the route was in cloud.

Final trials were conducted at the West Freugh Range from February until September 1972 on the LRMTS, which was to be fitted to the Harrier and Jaguar. Under a contract with Royal Aircraft Establishment, Farnborough, and utilising the Ferranti test pilot and flight test engineers, Canberra WJ643 now based at West Freugh and modified and equipped with the laser by RAE, was maintained by another contractor.

A revolutionary system followed some twenty-one years later in 1993, when the FFU at Turnhouse became momentarily resurrected, but in a drastically reduced size, for the purpose of developing the more advanced phased array scanner system, the ECR90, now flying in the Eurofighter 2000. In keeping with the philosophy of operating flight trials with easy access to the company, a military BAC1–11 (XE433), fitted with the system, operated about 300 flights from Turnhouse up until 2004, when another era of Turnhouse flight trials ended.

As many of the fighter/attack aircraft in the air forces of the western world are fitted with one or more of the systems or the derivatives designed and manufactured by the company, herein lies the legacy of the Ferranti Flying Unit at Turnhouse.

12
Scottish Fisheries

The Department of Agriculture and Fisheries for Scotland (DAFS), based in Edinburgh, were responsible for patrolling Scottish fishing waters and ascertaining that all fishing vessels were operating legally and were in their licensed locations. This watching brief mainly concerned foreign fishing vessels, but a 'paternal' eye was also kept on the Scottish fleet. The DAFS aircraft were also available in the event of an emergency. The aircraft have operated from Prestwick, Edinburgh, Aberdeen and Inverness. This section is concerned with the Edinburgh operation in the late 1980s. The aircraft were operated on behalf of the DAFS by Harvest Air of Southend, and the patrols were initially flown by a Dornier 228 (G–BNMD). The Do 228 was used on a trial basis for the four-year contract starting in 1986. However, after a year, it was decided that the aircraft was not suitable, and it was replaced by a Fokker F.27 (G–SOFS). This F.27 was originally built in 1959 and had seen service with Trans Australia Airlines, Air Niugini and by KLM (Cityhopper). It was modified by Air UK at Norwich in 1987, a modification which involved adding external wing tanks, centre-section bladder tanks and the installation of a Ferranti 'Seaspray' MkII search radar, which was tied in to a Litton LTN72R Inertial Navigation System. Beam windows were also fitted at the rear of the cabin. The F.27 was de-registered in December 1991, and later broken up at Southend.

The Offshore Patrol, as it was called, involved patrolling all areas more than 3 nautical miles offshore out until the median line (basically the halfway point between Scotland and where the nautical boundary of another country met the Scottish one). A patrol could cover up to 30,000sq. miles depending on weather conditions and fuel considerations. The patrols were more or less rotated right around the Scottish mainland on a weekly basis:

Monday: Patrol from Edinburgh out to the median line and north up to Orkney. Night stop at Kirkwall.
Tuesday: Patrol from Orkney to the east and north of Shetland. Night stop at Sumburgh.
Wednesday: Patrol to the west of Shetland north of Cape Wrath and down to the Butt of Lewis. Night stop at Stornoway.
Thursday: Take off from Stornoway, transit to Rockall area, patrol Rockall area, back to Stornoway and nightstop.

Do 228 G–BNMD. Picture taken in Madagascar. (Charlie Durnford)

Friday: Take off from Stornoway, patrol north to south down the Minches, climb out near Islay and transit back to Edinburgh. Go home for the weekend.

The following week, the second crew would take over, and might do the same pattern backwards. This varied depending on the time of year, on the location of the fishing fleets, on the breeding seasons and the weather patterns. The decisions were made by Scottish Fisheries Operations personnel, the crew merely following directions. An average patrol was between six and 7½ hours dependent on weather, number of fishing contacts and fuel.

Edinburgh was the point the patrol started from at the beginning of the week and returned to at the end, and was also convenient, as the Scottish Fisheries HQ was based in the city of Edinburgh. Also, as the crews came from all over the UK, Harvest Air bought a four-bedroom flat in Pilton which was used as accommodation when the crews were flying from Edinburgh.

The unit now operates from Inverness with two Reims Cessna F.406 Caravan aircraft as part of the Scottish Fisheries Protection Agency.

Do 228 G–BNMD. Another view of the aircraft and crew in Madagascar. (Charlie Durnford)

F.27 G–ASOFS in flight. The radar carried on this aircraft was the first sale of military radar by Ferranti to a civilian customer. (Charlie Durnford)

F.27 G–ASOFS before another patrol. (Charlie Durnford)

13
Eastern Lowlands University Air Squadron (ELUAS) and 12 Air Experience Flight (12 AEF)

At Turnhouse, the UAS and AEF had two separate roles, with the AEF providing air experience for members of the Combined Cadet Force, aged from thirteen to eighteen, and the UAS providing actual flying instruction from eighteen years upwards.

The Edinburgh University Air Squadron was formed in 1941 using RAF Turnhouse. Flying training took place in the Tiger Moth until the early 1950s when training was changed to the DH Chipmunk. In 1969 Heriott Watt University was added, and 1974 saw the addition of Stirling University. In 1975 the Chipmunks were replaced by the SA/BAE Bulldog. Napier College of Commerce and Technology (now Napier University) was also added to the squadron in 1979. At the closure of RAF Turnhouse in March 1996, the squadron (by now named ELUAS) transferred its operation to RAF Leuchars. With the transfer to Leuchars in 1996, the roles of the AEF and UAS became much more closely combined than they were at Turnhouse, and now operate as virtually one unit. In 2000 the Bulldogs were in turn replaced by Grob Tutors.

In 2003 the ESUAS (East of Scotland University Air Squadron) was formed at RAF Leuchars from the amalgamation of the ELUAS and ADStAUAS. The latter was made up from Aberdeen, Aberdeen Dundee and St Andrews University Air Squadrons. St Andrews had originally been absorbed into the East Lowlands UAS on 1 January 1969, but separated on 3 October 1981 to join with the Aberdeen and Dundee University squadrons.

Chipmunk WP967 of 12 Air Experience Flight (AEF). (Squadron Leader Bruce Blanche Collection)

'Farewell from RAF Turnhouse': a humorous view of 12 AEFs departure. (Gordon Sandford)

Appendix 1
Visiting/Viewing

The Spectators' Terrace is now closed and, unless you are in the departure area itself, nothing can be seen from the terminal. There are plenty of shops in the terminal, but there is decently priced, excellent food and drink served by two lovely ladies at Campsie Snacks just behind the BAE SYSTEMS hangar, near the General Aviation Terminal. As I have mentioned in the Sources/Bibliography section, for anyone just wishing to visit the airport for sightseeing or a day out, Martin Krupkas' website has a section by Gerry Hill which gives good locations for viewing and taking photographs, along with photographs of the locations themselves, which is very helpful. We live in changing times and watching aircraft has become an activity which is frowned upon by some authorities, but generally the police understand that there is an interest in aviation and I have found them to be accommodating if approached in the right manner.

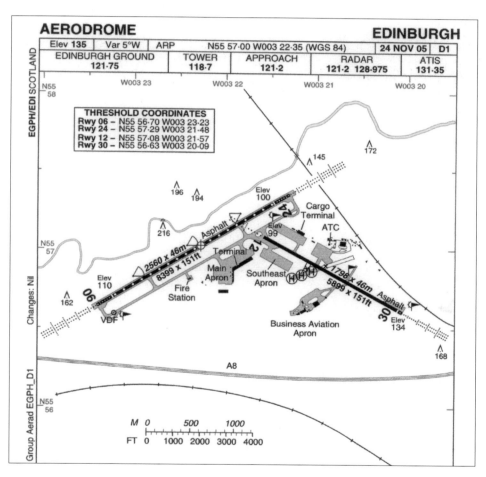

Edinburgh Airport Layout November 2005 (not for operational use). Due to magnetic variations the runway headings are 06/24 and 12/30 changed from 07/25 and 13/31 respectively. The latter headings are referred to in the text along with the now closed 08/26. (European Aeronautical Group UK Ltd)

Appendix 2
Air Transport Movements (ATMs) 1947–2004

Year	ATMs	Year	ATMs
1947	1,060	1976	19,951
1948	2,575	1977	29,583
1949	1,990	1978	21,848
1950	2,531	1979	26,649
1951	1,250	1980	26,681
1952	2,266	1981	23,945
1953	3,181	1982	25,609
1954	3,687	1983	28,616
1955	3,661	1984	33,166
1956	4,582	1985	36,926
1957	4,654	1986	36,596
1958	4,954	1987	39,603
1959	5,620	1988	40,664
1960	7,220	1989	47,100
1961	7,972	1990	47,900
1962	6,802	1991	49,700
1963	7,479	1992	56,400
1964	8,792	1993	58,800
1965	8,693	1994	61,100
1966	10,383	1995	64,000
1967	11,539	1996	68,800
1968	11,946	1997	71,700
1969	11,619	1998	75,400
1970	10,751	1999	83,600
1971	12,814	2000	87,900
1972	13,838	2001	99,100
1973	15,668	2002	105,800
1974	15,365	2003	106,200
1975	18,290	2004	112,500

The statistics are combined BAA & CAA figures, some of which have been rounded for ease of comparison. The BAA year runs from April to March and the CAA year is a calendar year.

Appendix 3
1947–2004 Passengers

Year	No.	Year	No.
1947	7,441★	1977	946,000
1950	21,300	1978	1,200,000
1951	13,800	1979	1,245,000
1952	28,200	1980	1,163,000
1953	37,900	1981	1,121,000
1954	45,800	1982	1,202,000
1955	63,000	1983	1,276,000
1956	89,600	1984	1,491,000

Year	No.	Year	No.
1957	107,900	1985	1,578,000
1958	111,500	1986	1,651,000
1959	149,300	1987	1,852,000
1960	213,400	1988	2,080,000
1961	259,700	1989	2,369,000
1962	318,000	1990	2,495,000
1963	389,800	1991	2,343,000
1964	444,100	1992	2,539,000
1965	489,100	1993	2,721,000
1966	531,200	1994	3,001,000
1967	600,000	1995	3,280,000
1968	616,000	1996	3,810,000
1969	602,000	1997	4,158,000
1970	653,000	1998	4,543,000
1971	681,000	1999	5,086,000
1972	755,000	2000	5,493,000
1973	878,000	2001	6,039,000
1974	790,000	2002	6,913,000
1975	874,000	2003	7,477,000
1976	823,000	2004	7,998,000

* 1948/1949 figures not available.

The statistics are combined BAA & CAA figures which have been rounded for ease of comparison. The BAA year runs from April to March and the CAA year is a calendar year.

Appendix 4
Scheduled Routes and Airlines (as at 30 November 2005)

Destination (domestic)	Airline
Belfast City Airport	Flybe
Belfast International	Easyjet
Birmingham	British Airways
	Flybe
	bmibaby
Bristol	Easyjet
	British Airways
Cardiff	bmibaby
Exeter	Flybe
Inverness	British Airways
Kirkwall	British Airways
Leeds/Bradford	bmi
Liverpool	Flybe
London City	British Airways
	Scot Airways
London Gatwick	British Airways
	Easyjet
London Heathrow	British Airways
	bmi

London Luton	Easyjet
London Stansted	FlyGlobespan
	Easyjet
Manchester	Jet2
	bmi
	British Airways
Norwich	Eastern Airways
	Flybe
Nottingham East Midlands	Easyjet
	bmibaby
Southampton	Flybe
	British Airways
Stornoway	British Airways
	bmi
Sumburgh	British Airways
Wick	British Airways

European	Airline
Alicante	FlyGlobespan
	Air Scotland
Amsterdam Schipol	KLM
	Easyjet
Barcelona El Prat	FlyGlobespan
Billund	British Airways
Brussels	bmi
Cologne/Bonn	Germanwings
Copenhagen	bmi
	Sterling (starts 1 March 2006)
Cork	Aer Arran
Dublin	Aer Lingus
	Ryanair
Faro	FlyGlobespan
Frankfurt International	Lufthansa
Galway	Aer Arran
Geneva	FlyGlobespan
	Easyjet (starts 15 December 2005)
Hamburg	Hapag-Lloyd Express
Helsinki	Finnair (starts 12 April 2006)
	Sterling
Ibiza	FlyGlobespan (starts 26 March 2006)
Madrid	British Airways
Malaga	FlyGlobespan
	Air Scotland
Milan Malpensa	British Airways
Munich	bmi (starts 27 March 2006)
Murcia	FlyGlobespan (starts 1 April 2006)
	Jet2 (starts 8 April 2006)
Nice	FlyGlobespan
Palma de Majorca	FlyGlobespan
Paris Charles de Gaulle	British Airways
	Air France

Prague	CSA Czech Airlines
Rome Leonardo da Vinci	British Airways
Stockholm Arlanda	SAS (starts 26 March 2006)
	Sterling (starts 3 March 2006)
Warsaw	Centralwings

Destination (international)	Airline
Atlanta	Delta Airways (starts 4 May 2006)
Moscow Domodedovo	Transaero
New York Newark	Continental
Orlando	Continental
Toronto Pearson	Air Transat

Charters: winter 2005/06 and summer 2006
Airlines

Thomsonfly, Monarch, Eurocypria, LTE, Iberworld, Helios, Onur Air, bmi, Pegasus, First Choice, Spanair, Futura, Nouvelair Tunisie, Air Europa, Mytravel, Flybe, BH Air.

Destinations

Alicante, Arrecife, Barcelona, Bastia, Bodrum, Chambery, Dalaman, Faro, Geneva, Ibiza, Innsbruck, Larnaca, Las Palmas, Mahon, Malaga, Monastir, Nice, Palma, Paphos, Plovdiv, Prague, Tenerife, Zakynthos.

Appendix 5
Ferranti Flying Unit Projects

Distance Measuring Equipment
Notorious
Blue Study
Airstream Direction Detector
Gyro Gun Sight Tracking
Single-seat Airborne Interception Radar A123/23B
Wyvern Strike Sight
Autostabilisation
Air to Surface Ranging Mk4
Pilot Attack Sight
Toss Bombing Computer
Yellow Jack
S-Band Homer
Red Brick
Buccaneer Strike Sight
Blue Parrot
Inertial Navigation and Attack System
Forward Looking Terrain Following Radar
Indigo Corkscrew
Laser Ranger and Marked Target Seeker
Eurofighter Phased Array Radar

All details courtesy of Len Houston, former chief test pilot, Ferranti Flying Unit, 1964 to 1973.

Appendix 6
Aircraft Allocated to Ferranti Flying Unit for Flight Trials

Douglas Dakota Mk3	TS423	15/08/49–13/10/67
Hawker Sea Fury T20	VX301	04/49–24/04/53
De Havilland Vampire FB	WG801	28/10/52–16/10/53
Fairey Gannet AS1	WE488	11/03/53–09/10/53
Vickers Valetta C1	VW145	24/03/53–mid 07/58
Hawker Sea Fury T20	VX283	09/05/53–26/09/53
Gloster Meteor T	VW470	28/12/53–08/10/56
Westland Wyvern S1	VW870	26/01/54–28/09/55
Gloster Meteor NF11/12	WD670	01/04/54–07/04/63
Fairey Gannet AS1	WN345	10/06/54–late 10/55
Gloster Meteor FR9	VW362	23/06/54–15/07/59
English Electric Canberra B2/B8	WJ643	07/09/54–31.03.69
Gloster Meteor FR9	VW360	25/08/55–10/02/58
Vickers Varsity T1	WJ937	07/09/55–11/10/55
English Electric Canberra B8	VX185★	30/04/56–16/10/56
English Electric Canberra B8	WT327	28/08/56–12/04/66
Hawker Hunter F4	WT736	16/11/56–19/11/58
Gloster Meteor NF11	WD790	22/05/58–23/05/67
Gloster Meteor NF11	WD782	28/10/58–06/09/60
English Electric Canberra B2	WJ627	04/08/59–09/09/63
English Electric Canberra B8	WJ787	28/10/59–02/12/63
Gloster Meteor NF14	G-ARCX(WM261)★★	15/09/60–14/08/73
English Electric Canberra SC9	XH139	30/05/61–14/09/61
English Electric Canberra B2	WD953	30/10/61–13/02/69
Blackburn Buccaneer NA39	XK487	07/05/63–04/04/66
English Electric Canberra B2	WD947	23/12/56–31/10/67
BAC 1–11	ZE433	1994–2004
HS 125 (Company Aircraft)	G–AXDM	

★ VX185 set a speed record on 26 August 1952 flying to Gander and back from Aldergrove in 10 hours and 3 minutes with one refuelling stop. The return segment took 3 hours and 25 minutes.
★★ Now exhibited at the Museum of Flight, East Fortune, East Lothian.

The following aircraft were allotted to Ferranti for Weapon System Trials and flown by the FFU Project Test Pilot for periodic trials:

Blackburn Buccaneer 1	XK523	(at RAE West Freugh)

At Warton from 1959–1965:

English Electric Lightning P1B	XG312
English Electric Lightning P1B	XG327
English Electric Lightning P1B	XG331
English Electric Lightning P1B	XG326
English Electric Lightning F3	XP964

All details courtesy of Len Houston (Ferranti Unit Chief Test Pilot, 1964–1973).

Appendix 7
Ferranti Pilots Flying on FFU Military Test Operations

E.K. Barnes	01/09/52–11/53
A.E. Featherstone	30/10/52–24/04/53
H.D. Shaw	11/52–26/09/53
P.J. Field	27/07/53–04/63
R.S. Flight	26/11/53–11/11/59
J. Pascoe–Watson	01/02/55–17/10/63
L.J.S. Houston	16/11/56–01/12/73
C.W. Curtis	30/09/59–05/05/64
J.J. Cockburn	12/04/61–28/07/66
R.E. Reeve	09/09/64–13/02/69

Post-Closure Phase

G. McIntosh	BAC 1–11
G. Delmege	BAC 1–11
B. Goddard	BAC 1–11
A. Mustard	BAC 1–11/HS 125

Ferranti Flight Test and Aircraft Engineers

Every effort has been made to update this list which represents the personnel who could be easily identified over some fifty-two years as contributing to flight test operations. It is regretted if there are some absent:

P. Gibson (first FTE, 1952); A. Thompson; J. Dowd; J. Simpson; D. Hale; S. Watts; N. Parker; J. Sutherland; J. Brotherston; P. Turnbull; L. Stevenson; W. Reid; J. Lawson; T. Casey; W. Roberts; T. Cochrane; T. McSorley; T. McCilwraith; T. Evett; D. Everest; C. Baxter; J. Chapman; J. Newbigging; G. Anderson; G. Stewart; J. Glover; B. Myddleton; J. Anderson; W. Forsythe; L. Butler.

Post-Closure Programmes

D. McAlpin; K. Martin; B. Patterson; G. Gilmour; P. McGinlay; I. Slaughter; P. Durham.
All details courtesy of Len Houston (Ferranti Unit Chief Test Pilot 1964–1973).

Appendix 8
Squadrons and Aircraft based
at RAF Turnhouse during the Second World War

603 (City of Edinburgh) Squadron	Supermarine Spitfire
141 Squadron	Boulton Paul Defiant
245 Squadron	Hawker Hurricane
253 Squadron	Hawker Hurricane
65 Squadron	Supermarine Spitfire
263 Squadron★	Westland Whirlwind
3 Squadron	Hawker Hurricane
607 Squadron	Hawker Hurricane
122 Squadron	Supermarine Spitfire

123 Squadron	Supermarine Spitfire
340 (Free French) Squadron	Supermarine Spitfire
341 (Free French) Squadron	Supermarine Spitfire
81 Squadron	Supermarine Spitfire
242 Squadron	Supermarine Spitfire
801 Squadron Fleet Air Arm	Hawker Sea Hurricane
822 Squadron Fleet Air Arm★	★ Grumman Martlet
884 Squadron Fleet Air Arm★★	Fairey Fulmar
808 Squadron Fleet Air Arm	Supermarine Seafire
807 Squadron Fleet Air Arm★★★	Supermarine Seafire
848 Squadron Fleet Air Arm	Grumman Avenger
886 Squadron Fleet Air Arm★	★ Supermarine Seafire and Spitfire VB/Hooked
895 Squadron Fleet Air Arm	Supermarine Seafire
63 Squadron (Reconnaissance)	North American Mustang
268 Squadron	North American Mustang
329 Squadron	Supermarine Spitfire

★ 263 Squadron Westland Whirlwinds were based at Drem but were frequent visitors to Turnhouse.
★★ Part of 13 Group.
★★★ Detachment.

The following squadrons have also been based at RFC/RAF Turnhouse for varying periods:

164 Squadron	26 Squadron (Detachment) B Flight
303 Squadron	151 Squadron
83 Squadron	84 Squadron (Can)
77 Squadron	89 Squadron (Can)
73 Squadron	36 Squadron
26 Reserve/Training Squadron	

Sources and Bibliography

Sources

Edinburgh Room, George IV Library, George IV Bridge, Edinburgh
There are many press cuttings referring to the airport and various air services to Edinburgh. There is also an original copy of the Norman & Dawbarn report kept here as well as a copy of Lord Rosebery's correspondence with the Ministry of Munitions. Also useful are minutes of meetings of the Lord Provosts Committee kept in year books with a very helpful and easy-to-use index.

British Airways Museum
Located in a small building in Viscount Way (just near Hatton Cross Roundabout), Heathrow – a treasure trove of BEA and BOAC memorabilia, including the posthumous George Cross awarded to BOAC Stewardess Barbara Harrison. Manned by enthusiastic and helpful volunteer staff, it is well worth a visit. Ring first for appointment: 0208 562 3124.

Fleet Air Arm Museum, RNAS Yeovilton, Somerset
The museum houses the Centre for Naval Aviation records and research, but cutbacks have led to a long waiting time (around one year) for queries to be dealt with. The staff are very helpful but have a large workload to deal with and it is better to make an appointment to conduct your own research there. Tel.: 01935 842635.

RAF Museum, Hendon, London
An excellent museum with a good archive section, run by knowledgeable and helpful staff.

Bibliography

The Greatest Squadron of Them All, vols I&II, by David Ross; Bruce Blanche; William Simpson (Grub Street, The Basement, 10 Chivalry Road, London SW11 1HT)
> This is the definitive history of 603 Squadron. It is unlikely to be equalled, let alone bettered.

Action Stations — 7: Military airfields of Scotland, the North-East and Northern Ireland, by David J. Smith (Haynes Sutton)
> A very brief history of RAF Turnhouse and Edinburgh Airport with emphasis on the military side.

Turnhouse: an object lesson, by The Rt Hon. The Earl of Rosebery
> The Earl had one hundred copies of the complete correspondence relating to his dispute with the Ministry of Munitions privately published. One copy is held by the National Library of Scotland.

Belfast International Airport: Aviation at Aldergrove since 1918, by Guy Warner; Jack Woods (Colourpoint Books)

Bournemouth International Airport, by Mike Phipp (Tempus Publishing Limited)

Prestwick Airport & Scottish Aviation, by Peter Berry MRaes (Tempus Publishing Limited)

'Report on a Land Airport for the City of Edinburgh', Norman & Dawbarn, 1937

Minutes of the Edinburgh Lord Provosts Committee Meetings 1939–1947

Air Britain

BAA Annual Report and Accounts 1969–2005

CAA UK Airport Traffic Statistics 1946–1973

Edinburgh Evening News

Edinburgh Dispatch

The Scotsman

Flight International

Air Pictorial

Useful websites and internet forums

I have made extensive use of the internet in my research. Even if the information required is not on the internet, you can easily find people who have the knowledge or can point you in the right direction. It is not a complete substitute for normal methods of research but it is a very powerful tool.

Websites

BKS – www.lineone.net/~biggles200
> Run by John Rowley. For all things BKS, this is the place to come.

Turnhouse – http://www.clourie.co.uk/turnhouse/index.html
> Run by Colin Lourie. Colin runs a very nostalgic and evocative site with many unique Turnhouse pictures, particularly of 1960s aircraft. The site also covers Renfrew, Abbbotsinch and Prestwick, and he is hoping to extend the coverage to more Scottish airports and airfields.

British Airways Museum – www.bamuseum.com
> See comments above.

Edinburgh Airport – www.users.zetnet.co.uk/jcurry/
> Run by Joe Curry. Despite my obvious bias, this is quite simply the best airport website I have come across on the internet. Joe's enthusiasm shines through and he has won an award for the site to prove how good it is!

RAF Northolt – www.fly.to/northolt/
> Run by Malcolm Lander. A comprehensive site covering RAF Northolt, with a number of interesting snippets of information.

Cambrian Airways – www.unforgettable.org.uk/cambrian/
> Run by Garry Hillard. Garry is a former Cambrian employee and, although the site is mainly

Cambrian Airways, it also covers Air Wales and Welsh Civil Aviation heritage. Garry is also hoping to cover British Eagle and Channel Airways at a later date.

77 Squadron – homepage.ntlworld.com/r_m_g.varley/77 Squadron Association.htm
Run by Mike Varley. Mike served in 77 Squadron and, along with Harry Shinkfield, they can answer any questions about the history of the squadron.

BAA Edinburgh – www.edinburghairport.com
The official BAA website which has up-to-date information on arrivals and departures and also a large number of up-to-date pictures of the airport can be accessed through this site.

Edinburgh Airport – egph.martinkrupka.cz
Run by Martin Krupka. A nice site with useful links plus a section by Gerry Hill on the best locations for taking photographs at the airport.

Edinburgh Airport – www.egph.net
Run by Robert Pittuck, who has kindly supplied some of the photographs for this book. More of his excellent pictures are on this site.

Edinburgh Airport – www.saap.co.uk
Run by Fred Seggie. A good site with many good Edinburgh pictures as well as pictures of Glasgow and Prestwick.

Northern Ireland Aviation – www.ulsteraviationsociety.co.uk
An active and knowledgeable society with many helpful and enthusiastic members is represented by this website.

www.airliners.net – Literally thousands upon thousands of photographs of aircraft, airports and other aviation-related subjects.

Internet forums

All these forums have very knowledgeable members on all aspects of aviation. With regard to aviation in Scotland it is most unlikely that any related question would remain unanswered by accessing all of them. There are some sites/forums which charge a fee but membership of all those referred to here is free.

www.taxiwayalpha.com
Founded by Gavin Coates. A good forum for Edinburgh devotees as well as for those looking for information on other Scottish airports.

www.airlinerworld.com
The Commercial forum has a strong Scottish contingent and excellent pictures are regularly posted. As the forum name suggests, it is concerned with modern commercial aircraft and also with airports.

www.pprune.org.uk
This is the 'Professional Pilots Rumour Network'. There are many very knowledgeable people on this forum.

www.scotavnet.com
This forum is under Yahoo groups. At first sight it appears to be mainly concerned with aircraft movements, serials and registrations at Scottish airports and airfields, but there is a wealth of Scottish aviation knowledge here.

www.theaerodrome.com
An unusual forum, in that it deals solely with aviation during the First World War.

Every attempt has been made to check the source of written and photographic material in this book and to gain copyright permission for its use. If a reader finds something they do not agree is the correct source, could they please contact me through the publisher.

Index

If you are interested in purchasing other books published by Tempus,
or in case you have difficulty finding any Tempus books in your local bookshop,
you can also place orders directly through our website

www.tempus-publishing.com